Talent Acquisition
and Attraction Explained

Talent Acquisition and Attraction Explained

Rebecca Lee

KoganPage

Publisher's note

Every possible effort has been made to ensure that the information contained in this book is accurate at the time of going to press, and the publishers and authors cannot accept responsibility for any errors or omissions, however caused. No responsibility for loss or damage occasioned to any person acting, or refraining from action, as a result of the material in this publication can be accepted by the editor, the publisher or the author.

First published in Great Britain and the United States in 2025 by Kogan Page Limited

Kogan Page
Kogan Page Ltd, 2nd Floor, 45 Gee Street, London EC1V 3RS, United Kingdom
Kogan Page Inc, 8 W 38th Street, Suite 902, New York, NY 10018, USA
www.koganpage.com

EU Representative (GPSR)
Authorised Rep Compliance Ltd, Ground Floor, 71 Baggot Street Lower, Dublin D02 P593, Ireland
www.arccompliance.com

Kogan Page books are printed on paper from sustainable forests.
© Kogan Page, 2025

ISBNs
Hardback   978 1 398 62436 8
Paperback   978 1 398 62437 5
Ebook   978 1 398 62438 2

British Library Cataloguing-in-Publication Data
A CIP record for this book is available from the British Library.

Typeset by Hong Kong FIVE Workshop, Hong Kong
Printed and bound by CPI Group (UK) Ltd, Croydon CR0 4YY

*To my incredible twins, George and India –
may you move through life with heart, humour and purpose.
Everything I do is, in some way, for you.*

*And to my late father – your strength, wisdom and the values
you lived by are the foundation I stand on. The Lee name
carries weight, and I'm proud to carry it forward.*

Contents

Preface

My name is Rebecca, and I've spent decades helping global businesses transform their approach to hiring – shifting from reactive recruitment to strategic, talent-first models at some of the world's most successful brands.

Like many in the recruitment profession, I stumbled into it by accident right after university, and I haven't looked back since.

What I love about talent acquisition (TA) is that it's both a science and an art. With the right strategy and data, you can shape powerful, scalable recruitment frameworks. But it's the storytelling – the human connection – that brings it all to life. Great TA is about more than filling roles. It's about connecting people with purpose and helping organizations grow through their people.

There's nothing more rewarding than being part of someone's career journey, and nothing more impactful for a business than getting the right talent in place.

I wrote this book with early-career HR and talent professionals in mind, because I'm passionate about developing the next generation of talent leaders. I hope what you find here gives you practical insight, a few new ways of thinking and the confidence to lead with clarity and purpose.

About the author

Rebecca Lee is a global leader in talent transformation, award-winning recruitment strategist and co-founder of TA Innovation Hive – an online global community for TA leaders. With over 25 years of experience at organizations including Ericsson, JP Morgan, EY, Transport for London and Synopsys, she has led large-scale teams and pioneered innovative approaches in employer branding, early careers, digital learning, talent and onboarding.

Named one of the 'Top 5 Most Innovative Women in Talent Acquisition', she is known for blending strategic vision with authentic, people-first leadership. Her thought leadership features regularly in industry media and global conferences, and she's a passionate advocate for early-career development.

In this debut, she shares practical insights and personal lessons from her career journey – offering inspiration and guidance for the next generation of talent professionals.

Introduction

Introducing talent acquisition

This book has been written with early career human resources (HR) and talent acquisition (TA) professionals in mind. It is designed to help you have strategic conversations and navigate the art and science of recruitment with confidence – and yes, recruitment is a science, with a little bit of art thrown in. It will embolden you as an early career HR and/or TA professional to learn best practices and apply the learning to your organization. It will also be useful for aspiring HR Business Partners who hope to bridge the gap between HR and business strategy.

If you're reading this, you're likely new to HR, involved in talent acquisition, or aspiring to be in an HR/TA role. You may have experienced a poor hiring process yourself. This book will encourage you to reflect on your experience and apply learning. What worked well? What could have been improved? By exploring these questions, you'll gain valuable insights into how recruitment can be enhanced in the future.

By the end of the book, you will hopefully be able to demonstrate that recruitment is both an art and a science.

Why this book is different

What is the key to the future of your company? Or more importantly, who is the key to the future of your company, and how do you ensure that you identify, attract, retain and develop their potential?

Identifying, attracting, retaining, and developing top talent is not just an HR activity – it's a business imperative. Senior executives consistently agree that talent is a core competitive advantage. Yet, despite this consensus, recruitment practices often remain undervalued, underinvested and disconnected from strategic priorities.

Today, we're operating in a world defined by two major shifts:

1 Talent is now borderless. The best people can work from anywhere, and expect freedom and flexibility.
2 Businesses are now digital. Agility, data, and speed shape competitive advantage more than size and scale.

In this new landscape, traditional hiring practices, built for predictable environments and bygone eras, are no longer sufficient. Many organizations are stuck using reactive and transactional hiring methods, which are disconnected from strategic intent.

Organizations must therefore evolve their recruitment capabilities to match this new reality. This means adopting a more mature and strategic approach to TA, one that's proactive, data-informed and aligns hiring with business growth. Hiring talent must lead business strategy. In the past, many hiring efforts were based on gut feeling, or intuition, but this will no longer suffice in the modern world. Placing talent at the heart of your business strategy now requires a complete transformation in how most companies approach hiring.

This book will help you navigate the complex world of hiring and help you develop your career so that you can lead the transition from reactive to strategic TA. As you do this, two questions are vital to keep at the forefront of your mind:

1 How can we recruit, utilize, and develop people to deliver greater value to customers, and outperform competition?

2 How can I know that I have the right approach to TA to drive the changes that we need?

As a new HR or TA practitioner, this book will encourage you to pose these challenging questions to your leadership team, sparking deeper conversations around talent, and elevating expectations around talent acquisition. It will show you what it takes to drive these discussions and push TA forward. While the idea that people generate value is simple, helping your organization understand the need to become a talent-first organization is nuanced and harder.

This book will help you grow into an HR or TA practitioner with the skills and understanding to transform your company, whether it's a fast-growing start-up, scale-up or global organization, to one that recognizes the value of hiring and putting people first. In doing this, you will elevate HR and TA, and your own career success.

Throughout the book, you will find a range of reflection points, tips and practical exercises, all of which are designed to help you discover insights, apply your learning to your own organizational context and take action. Not every exercise will necessarily be relevant to your current role and responsibilities; you should undertake the ones that you feel are most relevant to you and your role or the direction you wish to pursue in your future career. The book also has many real-world examples to help cement your learning. Each chapter ends with review questions to test your learning and understanding. Use the endnotes to discover more about any research, reports or publications from other organizations discussed throughout.

Some reflection questions are called 'What would you do?'. These ask you to reflect on what you would do in specific scenarios. There are not necessarily any 'right' answers to these exercises. Think about what you would do, using the content in the chapter when necessary to determine your answer. After you have had a chance to reflect, you can then visit the Appendix, where you will find suggested answers.

The structure of this book

The book begins by looking at how TA has evolved from ancient times to now, placing diversity, equity, and inclusion at the heart of recruitment and showing how it is far from a modern consideration. Chapter 2 looks at the mindset and capability you will need to be a strategic practitioner working in TA, explaining why this is necessary and outlining the skills you will need to succeed.

Chapter 3 introduces the 12 modern building blocks of TA. These are the fundamental elements that make up a TA function, which can be adapted to suit smaller organizations that incorporate TA into the broader HR function, and organizations at the very beginning of developing more sophisticated recruitment practices. It aligns the building blocks with the well-known TA lifecycle, showing the relationship between the two. These building blocks form the structure for the rest of the book, with each of the chapters looking at one of the functional blocks in turn.

First, Chapter 4 looks at workforce planning and recruitment forecasting, an element of TA that needs to happen before anything else. It's a truly scientific element of TA. Chapter 5 considers the importance of a strong employer brand, and demonstrates how everything in the TA lifecycle flows from it. It's the lynchpin of engaging prospective employees, and getting it wrong can have dire consequences for an organization. Chapter 6 moves on to candidate attraction and sourcing – the next functional TA building block. It looks at innovative ways to attract and source top talent, drawing on as wide a talent pool as possible and ensuring you are attracting diverse candidates. Chapter 7 looks at assessment and selection, considering aspects such as common pitfalls, different methods and tools and how to ensure fairness and reduce bias in the process. Finally, Chapter 8 looks at our last TA building block – onboarding and retention. We consider how onboarding should be a TA activity and include early development of candidates to ensure their success within the company. Last but not least, the Conclusion considers the future of TA, especially in relation to AI and what it means for your career.

CHAPTER ONE

The evolution of TA

Introduction

This chapter introduces the history of talent acquisition (TA) from ancient civilizations to the present day. Some of what you read in this chapter might surprise you. Practices we may think of as 'modern', such as diversity, equity, and inclusion, have, in fact, been around for thousands of years. As contemporary TA practitioners, this helps us to understand that we are not doing something new – we are continuing a legacy that has existed for millennia.

Despite all the advancements in technology and organizational strategy, diversity, equity, and inclusion (DEI) remain persistent and complex challenges. Even with dedicated teams and growing awareness, the work is far from finished, and progress in TA is slower than it should be.

We begin by looking at the origins of organized hiring, particularly the lessons we can learn from equitable hiring practices in the past. We look at how historical practices have evolved into TA as we know it today – often a distinct function with several elements. We progress to look at how societal, economic and technological shifts have influenced the evolution of TA, and how they are set to continue doing so at an unprecedented pace. With the rate of technological change today, it is important to keep human and ethical considerations at the heart of our hiring strategies, and we look at how to do this, alongside a real-world example of what could happen if we take our eye off the ball.

Overall, this chapter explains how recruitment is a powerful lever for progress, shaping who gets opportunities, and how talent is valued and accessed.

LEARNING OBJECTIVES

By the end of this chapter, you will be able to:

- Explain how hiring practices have changed throughout history, why they matter today and how they shape modern hiring strategies.

- Articulate the importance of creating fair, flexible, and business-aligned recruitment processes that prioritize diversity.

- Identify the core HR problem-solving skills necessary to stay ahead in the face of ongoing societal, economic, and technological impacts on recruitment.

- Understand the evolving role of HR as an integral partner in TA, emphasizing collaboration, technology adoption, and continuous improvement.

Why TA goes beyond just filling roles

Talent acquisition: The process of identifying, attracting, and hiring skilled individuals to meet an organization's needs, with a strategic, long-term mindset.

Recruitment: The process of filling immediate vacancies as they arise, with a reactive, short-term mindset.

In this book, you'll see the terms recruitment and talent acquisition (TA) used interchangeably; however, they are subtly different. So, why the distinction? What exactly is TA, how does it differ from traditional recruitment, and what does the journey to get to where we are today look like?

While recruitment typically refers to simply filling positions, TA goes beyond simply filling positions, and refers to a strategic, long-term approach to identifying, attracting, and building sustainable talent pipelines to retain talent while fostering a great employer brand. It's about planning, engaging with potential candidates over time, and creating an inclusive culture that enhances the overall employee experience. This distinction is important, as many companies, regardless of size, still operate with a traditional recruitment-focused model, reacting to staffing needs as they arise. The most successful organizations, however, have evolved into TA, adopting a more strategic, forward-thinking approach to attracting and retaining top talent.

The origins of organized hiring

While the term 'talent acquisition' itself may sound modern, the practice of recruitment has evolved over centuries, shaped by economic, social and technological changes. Recruitment is one of humanity's oldest professions, deeply intertwined with the rise of civilizations. From sourcing skilled labour for ancient monuments to organizing armies for battle, the practice of finding and allocating talent has been a cornerstone of human progress. Recruitment today is a foundational element of HR, but is far older than HR as a formalized discipline, and has existed independently for millennia.

Today, recruitment resides within the HR function as a centre of excellence (CoE) and plays a critical role in supporting HR's broader remit. As an early career professional in HR or TA, it's important to understand how recruitment has evolved, as it provides context for modern TA strategies and challenges and helps you to recognize some of the historic practices still evident today. This knowledge will empower you to guide your organization towards proactive recruitment. From empires to modern systems, the key principles and definition of recruitment have proved timeless, and the fundamental goal remains the same: *hiring the right people for the right roles, in the right place, at the right time.*

Equitable hiring practices throughout history

Diversity is an important theme throughout this book. Building inclusive and diverse workforces should be at the centre of any TA strategy. But contrary to what many people think, it is not a twentieth-century concept. Throughout history, societies have grappled with issues of inclusion, representation, and equity – themes that continue to shape modern workforce strategies. For example, recruitment was crucial in shaping the Roman Empire (27 BCE to 476 CE). The Romans developed structured systems to enlist citizens into the military. They didn't just want to fill positions; they aspired to strategically attract and retain talent by offering powerful incentives such as land and citizenship to entice individuals to join and stay. The connection between recruitment and reward systems laid the groundwork for systems we use today to motivate, retain, and engage employees, such as compensation, benefits, and incentives.

Similarly, the Tang Dynasty in China (618–907 CE) is often credited with formalizing and expanding the Imperial Examination system, which democratized opportunity by enabling civil servants to be selected based on merit rather than family background. This was done by providing Confucian texts to help applicants prepare for the Imperial Examinations, effectively levelling the playing field and seeing individuals hired from more diverse backgrounds based on their ability rather than social status or privilege. This concept mirrors modern diversity and inclusion efforts, and even by today's standards would be considered transformative.

Today, many forward-thinking UK public sector organizations, such as the NHS and civil service, continue this ancient legacy by providing applicants with an upfront list of competencies to be assessed in the application process, alongside interview preparation materials. The Big Four professional service accountancy firms, which compete fiercely for top graduate and school leaver talent, also embrace similar meritocratic hiring methodologies. For example, in 2015, Ernst & Young (EY) in the UK became the first of the major accountancy firms to remove academic degree classifications (such as the traditional 2:1 requirement) from its graduate programme eligibility criteria. Instead, it introduced numeric ability tests and strengths-based assessments to evaluate candidates. The company found no correlation between higher education success and future professional performance. PricewaterhouseCoopers (PwC) followed suit, loosening its graduate recruitment criteria and removing the mandatory 2:1 degree requirement for many roles. This reinforced a shift toward a more inclusive and skills-based approach to hiring.

Some smaller organizations also weave in similar open practices today, by providing interview questions ahead of time to candidates who require reasonable adjustments (e.g. those who are neurodivergent).

> **Skills-based hiring:** A concept based on hiring for skills, abilities and potential, rather than traditional qualifications like academic degrees.

> **Reasonable adjustments:** Modifications applied to the recruitment process aimed at removing or reducing any disadvantages experienced by individuals with a declared disability. This ensures they have equal access to opportunities. An example of a legitimate reasonable adjustment is providing extra time for students with dyslexia during an online graduate testing process.

TOP TIP

Be curious about history

History can show you what works and why, and help you challenge hiring managers who are reluctant to adopt forward-thinking approaches such as merit-based hiring. (We cover the hiring manager relationship in Chapter 2.)

Creating inclusive, adaptable recruitment systems

Understanding the historical evolution of recruitment offers valuable insights into shaping the future. It's essential to ensure that diversity, equity, and inclusion remain at the forefront of all hiring practices. As each era brings new workforce challenges and opportunities, HR professionals must be agile, forward-thinking, and committed to driving meaningful, sustainable progress.

Despite centuries of evolution, diversity hiring remains a persistent and unresolved issue. Organizations continually strive to create truly inclusive systems that ensure opportunities for underrepresented groups, reflecting the same aspirations seen as far back as ancient times. Diversity is a golden thread woven through history, still shaping the talent landscape today. All too often, the aspiration has been hindered by deep-rooted obstacles and ingrained biases.

The continual quest for equity and diversity drives innovation and progress across industries. Modern tools, like AI-driven assessments and sophisticated methods like blind hiring and CV-free hiring using data-driven selection, aim to reduce bias. Yet systemic barriers persist, from disparities in education and professional and parental networks to gaps in digital literacy. These challenges reflect the complexities of creating environments where diverse talent can thrive, evolving constantly to meet the needs of a global workforce.

AI-driven assessments: A way of assessing candidates that uses algorithms to enhance such things as skills tests and psychometric testing.

Blind hiring: When identifying information (e.g. name, school, university, post code) is removed from a candidate's application to reduce unconscious bias during the early stages of hiring.

Data-driven selection: A process of making decisions, especially in hiring, that are based on objective, quantifiable data rather than subjective options or personal preferences. The goal is to set consistent criteria supported by evidence to guide selection decisions. CV-free hiring eliminates the traditional CV/résumé altogether and candidates are evaluated through predefined tests, simulations or scenario-based exercises that generate quantifiable results – removing subjectivity.

Building a truly inclusive workforce goes beyond simply providing access to roles; it requires actively fostering an environment where diverse talent can feel belonging and thrive. This means challenging outdated norms, embracing ambiguity, and creating solutions that can respond to the complexities of a rapidly changing world. This change is often brought on by societal, economic and technological shifts, which we will consider in the next section.

EXERCISE

How does your organization incorporate diversity and inclusion into its hiring practices? Use the following questions to help you audit the current situation.

1   Assess current diversity and inclusion practices.

   ○   Review how diversity and inclusion are embedded into existing
       hiring practices. Talk to your manager and other colleagues.

   ○   Are there any formal diversity and inclusion strategies,
       policies, or programmes in place?

2   Evaluate the focus on ability and potential, rather than relying
    on traditional criteria such as academic attainment.

   ○   Do hiring managers focus on skills and potential, particularly
       for entry-level roles?

   ○   Do hiring managers overly rely on academic attainment and
       qualifications?

   ○   Do hiring managers always ask for past industry
       experience?

   ○   Are there examples of skills-based hiring practices, or bold
       practices like those in the UK civil service or other
       progressive organizations?

3   Consider supportive interview processes.

   ○   Are candidates offered interview preparation materials as
       reasonable adjustments?

   ○   Can these resources be enhanced, or more widely accessible
       for greater inclusivity, for example, group exercise extracts
       at an assessment centre?

4   Stretch challenge: Embracing progressive hiring approaches.

   ○   Has your organization begun implementing skills-based
       hiring practices, such as:

       −   Blind recruitment?

       −   CV-free applications?

       −   Creating an internal marketplace and career pathways?

       −   Are you ready to test or scale bolder approaches to build
           a more inclusive, and meritocratic talent pool?

How society, economics and technology shape TA

One of the most challenging aspects of any HR or TA professional's role is adjusting recruitment strategies quickly in response to external factors which are often beyond an organization's control.

Businesses operate in dynamic environments, balancing operating costs and business growth, often in challenging conditions brought about by societal, economic and technological shifts. From the industrial era, when hiring focused on low-skill, high-output labour driven by economic prosperity, to today's digital and technological age, the nature of work has continuously evolved.

As the world changes, new challenges emerge, requiring HR professionals to adapt and respond by rethinking traditional hiring models and developing innovative solutions to support the business achieve its goals. Often, these shifts are unanticipated, and they can have wide-ranging impacts on the workforce. Both HR and TA professionals must learn to navigate these external influences to help their businesses stay competitive.

HR and TA are often criticized for being too 'internally' focused, with insufficient awareness of what is happening outside the organization. Societal, economic and technological forces are continuing to reshape the workforce, and TA needs to predict these, and be agile to help the business adapt to new models of working, evolving hiring practices, and ensuring equitable access to opportunities.

As a result, HR needs to recognize that building a truly inclusive workforce goes beyond simply providing access to roles; it requires actively fostering an environment where diverse talent can feel belonging and thrive. This means challenging outdated norms, embracing ambiguity, and creating solutions that can respond to the complexities of a rapidly changing world. It means providing a level playing field to underrepresented groups by removing recruitment barriers and offering equal opportunities to grow.

Societal shifts

The Covid-19 pandemic is an example of a societal shift that revolutionized recruitment, redefining how and where talent is sourced. Accelerating the shift towards remote and, now, hybrid work, it enabled companies to tap into global talent pools and embrace borderless hiring in a very short space of time. While this offered unprecedented opportunities for organizations to access a broader pool of talent, it also disrupted traditional recruitment systems, forcing companies to pivot rapidly to fully digital recruiting formats and navigate a talent landscape that is more complex than ever.

Practices that had previously been in-person, such as interviews and assessments, were reimagined at scale, with every company having to move to virtual and fully digital methods. Some smaller firms were able to respond with relative agility, but many larger graduate employers that hire in large volumes struggled with this disruptive change, as it required a completely new skill set for TA professionals.

Beyond expanding the talent pool, these shifts underscored the growing importance of technology, agility, and adaptability in HR. As the pandemic subsided, hybrid models emerged, blending in-person and digital processes. This 'new normal' demands that organizations rethink past strategies, balancing the flexibility and cost-effectiveness of virtual methods with the need for personal interaction.

Recruitment and HR teams must now be multi-skilled to manage these parallel hybrid processes effectively. As TA evolves, businesses must strike the right balance between technology and human connection to deliver a seamless, inclusive, and effective recruitment experience for both candidates and employers.

STOP AND THINK

Reflect on the pandemic and the challenges your organization now faces moving from remote to hybrid working. How have

> recruitment strategies been impacted alongside candidate
> expectations and the demand for greater work–life balance shifts
> and flexible working?

Economic trends

Economic shifts can compel organizations to rethink their hiring strategies in an instant. Local economic changes, such as shifts in government, taxation, or fiscal policy, can directly impact recruitment budgets and hiring decisions. Global economic fluctuations, such as the 2007 Global Financial Crisis or the Covid-19 pandemic, often trigger uncertainty, leading to hiring freezes, budget reductions, stricter labour cost controls, or even redundancies.

These pressures can limit TA efforts and intensify competition for available roles, demanding that HR professionals remain agile and strategic. Ultimately, economic changes play a critical role in shaping the supply and demand for talent. During periods of economic downturn, layoffs and hiring freezes often create an oversupply of candidates, resulting in intensified competition for fewer positions. This is known as an 'employer-driven' market as employers are in control. They have a large pool of candidates to pick from and the flexibility to set the terms of employment – they can offer lower salaries or fewer benefits without fear of losing candidates. Recruitment becomes more operationally challenging due to the overwhelming surge in applications, requiring more time and resources to effectively screen candidates. In an employer-led market, TA tends to become more process-driven and reactive, focusing on efficiency and compliance, rather than strategy.

Conversely, during periods of economic growth or recovery, demand for talent often outpaces supply, creating a 'candidate-driven market'. In these conditions, candidates have the upper hand as there are more job openings than qualified candidates to fill them. There can be a surge in hiring activity, but a simultaneous decline in both the volume and quality of applicants. This mismatch fuels a buoyant and competitive recruitment landscape, where employers must work harder to attract and retain top talent. They may need to offer more attractive compensation packages, benefits, flexible work options and career development opportunities. They may also need to invest in employer brand initiatives to differentiate their brand and stand out in a competitive job market (for more on employer branding, refer to Chapter 5). During these times, TA becomes the lifeblood of the organization.

Employer-driven market: Times when the supply of candidates exceeds the demand for talent, meaning there are more candidates seeking jobs than available positions.

Candidate-driven market: Times when the demand for talent exceeds the supply, giving job seekers more power and control over the hiring process.

The Covid-19 pandemic clearly illustrated this pattern, with an initial focus on cost efficiency followed by an intensified shift in skills demand. During the early phase of the pandemic, many organizations implemented furloughs (a temporary leave of absence or reduction in hours), hiring freezes, or shutdowns as they faced uncertainty and financial strain. However, as businesses adapted to remote work and digital transformation, the economy reopened, triggering a post-pandemic hiring surge, particularly for organizations that sought new digital skills. This shift emphasized the importance of agility in recruitment strategies, as companies pivoted to meet the evolving demands of the workforce.

These economic changes often drive HR and technological advancements, shaping how organizations adapt their hiring strategies for the future. Unfortunately, this is often why recruitment tends to be short-term and reactive, as economic conditions can shift rapidly.

As an HR professional, you can advise your organization on how to scale recruitment efforts up and down in response to sudden economic changes, such as downturns, hiring freezes, or talent shortages during periods of rapid growth.

Technology disruption

Technological change is accelerating, with breakthroughs occurring at an unprecedented pace. These technological shifts can be traced right back to the industrial era, which introduced more structured approaches to recruitment. In the twentieth century, the rise of technology companies heightened the demand for skilled workers, leading to further formalization of hiring practices and the introduction of technology platforms which connected job seekers with employers on a global scale. The rise of Applicant Tracking Systems (ATS) streamlined hiring by automating resume screening and candidate tracking, while in the early twenty-first century, job boards and online marketplaces (for example, LinkedIn, Indeed and Glassdoor) reshaped hiring.

> **Applicant Tracking Systems:** Technology that helps businesses manage the recruitment and hiring process for tracking purposes.

Today, artificial intelligence (AI) is driving another wave of profound change, pushing organizations to embrace technology faster than ever anticipated. AI is poised not just to enhance processes but to drive innovation itself. In recruitment, this transformation is already underway, reshaping how we source, assess, and hire talent. But it's a double-edged sword. On one hand, AI brings remarkable efficiencies, streamlining candidate sourcing and automating repetitive tasks. On the other, it presents new challenges, with the most pressing being the overwhelming volume of applications generated by AI-driven systems. Candidates can now apply to hundreds of jobs with a single click, making it harder for companies to identify top talent amidst the flood of submissions.

This influx of AI-generated applications is a new and unprecedented challenge for TA teams. With a limited number of positions to fill, the sheer volume of applications can quickly overwhelm recruitment processes, leading to delays, poor communication with candidates, and a lack of transparency. These negative experiences not only affect how candidates perceive the organization, they can also damage the company's employer brand and undermine long-term hiring success.

STOP AND THINK

How has your organization adapted to technological evolution since Covid-19 and the rise of AI?

- Has your organization embraced any emerging tools to reshape HR and recruitment or is it more risk-averse?
- If it has, are you facing any challenges integrating AI tools?
- What changes have you noticed in your team's daily work since AI or automation starting playing a more significant role?

THE IMPORTANCE OF A HUMAN-CENTRIC AND ETHICAL APPROACH

In this environment, it's more important than ever for TA teams to balance efficiency with empathy. The challenge is to ensure a smooth and transparent experience that aligns with the company's values, without replacing the human touch that fosters meaningful connections. AI can drive efficiencies, but it shouldn't come at the expense of a human-centric approach to recruitment.

HR professionals must also be vigilant and carefully evaluate how AI and technology are harnessed to ensure fairness, transparency, and equity in hiring, while safeguarding their ethical use by addressing bias, protecting privacy, and keeping human oversight in place. Two of the biggest challenges with the use of ethical AI in recruitment are bias and data privacy concerns.

1 **Bias**

   The following Amazon real-world example highlights how AI systems can learn patterns based on historical data, which may reflect past biases. If the training data used to build an AI tool is biased (e.g. favouring one gender, race, or educational background), it may perpetuate hidden biases in the recruitment process and lead to an adverse outcome for those from disadvantaged backgrounds. It's therefore important that AI is trained on diverse and inclusive data. Human oversight is upheld at critical decision points throughout the recruitment process to ensure fairness in candidate selection.

2 **Data privacy concerns**

   Using AI in recruitment involves processing sensitive personal data, such as resumes, interview recordings and psychometric assessments. HR professionals must ensure compliance with data protection regulations, including the European Union's General Data Protection Regulation (GDPR). AI systems that collect and store candidate data need to operate transparently, providing clear information about how data is used and ensuring that candidates can give informed consent for the processing of their data. Candidates have the right to an explanation when automated decision-making is used.

As we move toward an AI-driven future in recruitment, TA and HR professionals need to act as guardians of both ethical and legal standards, ensuring that AI serves to enhance – not hinder the integrity of hiring. We consider this point more in the Conclusion to this book.

Ethical AI: A way of using AI in recruitment that ensures fairness, integrity, transparency and the protection of individuals' privacy and rights.

REAL-WORLD EXAMPLE
Learning from Amazon's mistakes

In 2018, Amazon was eager to embrace cutting-edge AI technology and solidify its position as an industry-leading technology pioneer. However, it had to abandon an AI-driven recruitment tool after discovering it was biased against women. The system, designed to automate résumé screening, was trained on historical hiring data from the past decade; this training data largely reflected an already male-dominated tech workforce.

As a result, the AI unintentionally penalized résumés containing terms like 'women's' (e.g. 'women's chess club') while favouring language more commonly associated with male candidates. Despite efforts to correct these biases, it scrapped the AI experimental tool, which was never used in live hiring decisions, because Amazon's internal testing raised enough concerns that the project was ultimately abandoned.

This case highlights a fundamental risk of AI in recruitment: when trained on biased historical data, even the most advanced algorithms can reinforce existing systematic inequalities rather than eliminate them. The Amazon case is often cited as a key example of why human oversight is critical in AI-driven hiring; without it, AI can reinforce existing biases that are already in the workforce.

TOP TIP
Adopt an external focus

As an HR professional, it's crucial to understand your business's external environment and key challenges. The earlier you start to do this in your career, the better, as it will become second nature. Anticipating how economic, technological, and political factors will impact your organization and recruitment strategy will set you apart.

- Start by evaluating your current economic climate. Are budget constraints, hiring freezes, or inflation affecting your ability to hire effectively?

- Now, look at the role technology plays in your recruitment process. Are you using recruitment automation to streamline operations, and are these technologies being used in a way that aligns with ethical standards of fairness?

- Next, stay updated on any political or global events that impact regulatory requirements. How are changes in labour laws or tax policies impacting your ability to hire effectively?

By understanding these external pressures, you will become a better business partner, proactively adapting your recruitment approach to the candidate or employer-driven market, and ensuring it's flexible, cost-effective, and in line with your organization's evolving needs.

WHAT WOULD YOU DO?
Number 1

As an HR professional in a scale-up business, your TA team is managing over 1,000 applications to support business growth and global expansion plans. The business has requested to hire 50 new technology software engineers across 10 regions with some urgency.

The company is male-dominated and also wants to increase diversity in the hiring process. With just three weeks to complete interviews, and other roles to manage, manual screening is not feasible. Given the high volume, your TA team decides to use AI to scan résumés in real time, filtering candidates based on academic attainment and technical skills. However, human review still takes at least 10 minutes per candidate, making full manual screening impractical.

While the team plans to rely entirely on AI, you believe human oversight is essential at the screening stage and in deciding which candidates should move to the interview stage. How do you make your case?

CHAPTER SUMMARY

- Recruitment isn't new. It's one of the oldest human practices. Long before HR became a function, civilizations like the Ancient Egyptians, Roman Empire and Tang Dynasty created structured systems to find the right people for important roles, like soldiers or civil servants.

- Some modern hiring practices, like offering candidate preparation or hiring for potential, have been around in some form for centuries. Historical recruitment may even have been more inclusive than what we see today; it's not a modern-day trend, but a legacy.

- Recruitment flexes in line with societal, economic and technological changes. This evolution is ongoing, with AI set to drive another wave of profound change and present unprecedented challenge to professionals working in TA. It's crucial to stay adaptable.

- The Covid-19 pandemic reshaped how we recruit: remote interviews, hybrid assessment centres and global talent pools became the norm. HR now needs to balance tech with a human touch and always keep equity at the centre.

REVIEW QUESTIONS

1 Why is it important to judge candidates on skills and potential, rather than relying solely on academic grades and prior experience?

2 What happens in a candidate-led market? What challenges and strategies might HR or TA face when recruiting, and how can they adapt to attract top talent?

3 What potential risks could organizations face when implementing AI recruitment tools using test or training data?

CHAPTER TWO

The mindset and capability for strategic TA

Introduction

When working in HR or TA, especially early in your career, it can sometimes be difficult to get off the 'hamster wheel of delivery' and take a step back, away from low-value activities and obediently responding to constant business demands.

To progress in your career, it's vital to take time to pause and reflect, anticipate, influence and guide with intention. In other words, it's crucial to work towards becoming a strategic business partner. While you will inevitably begin your career with a tactical delivery focus, knowing how to ask the right questions and shift towards a more strategic mindset will set you on an exciting path to leadership in HR and/or TA.

In this chapter, we explore how you can develop the mindset and capability to become a strategic, trusted partner, whether you're supporting TA as an HR practitioner or working within a TA team. We focus on the partnership with hiring managers, as they are TA's key customers.

We begin by looking at why shifting from transaction to strategic TA is important, both for the organization and for your career growth. We pay particular attention to the role of the HR Business Partner (HRBP). We look at how to access an organization's talent maturity through the lens of the hiring manager, before focusing on managing conversations with stakeholders, saying 'no' to low-value requests and building strong relationships to foster alignment and earn long-term trust.

To succeed in TA, there are certain core skills you will need. We look at a taxonomy of skills for TA as well as some practical scenarios for how to apply them. We end the chapter by looking at the metrics that matter and ways to elevate the hiring manager's experience to make better decisions and stronger hires.

Whether you're in HR or TA, this chapter aims to give you practical tools, examples and language that help you move from reacting to requests to shaping the strategy.

LEARNING OBJECTIVES

By the end of this chapter, you will be able to:

- Understand the shift from transactional to strategic TA.
- Assess the talent maturity of your organization.
- Have courageous HR conversations with stakeholders.
- Embed a modern TA and HR skill set to thrive.
- Select which metric to track to gain insight into specific TA questions.
- Elevate the hiring manager experience for better decision-making and stronger hires with insight and impact.

Shifting from transactional to strategic TA

This book is written for those in typical HR roles at the start of their career, as well as for those working within TA teams in the early stages of their career. This chapter is largely aimed at those in HR who need to establish clear parameters of the scope of their role and how they might support TA. In larger organizations, your role in HR is likely to become the connective tissue linking leadership, TA, other HR centres of excellence and employees. Amanda Rajkumar, board CHRO (former Executive Board Member and Chief People Officer at adidas), said at a recruitment event: 'The HR business partner teams are the main relationship managers bringing the deal team together between TA, reward, and talent development to support the business.' You will support TA to elevate its voice, impact and influence. In smaller organizations, the responsibility lines blur a little more. Your role might span both HR and TA and may involve stepping into the front line of recruitment delivery yourself. The guidance in this chapter can be applied to either scenario.

In larger organizations, a potential career route if you are in HR is to become an HR Business Partner (HRBP).

TOP TIP
Lean into your passions

To help you start thinking strategically, pick the element of the TA lifecycle that you feel most passionate about (we delve into the TA lifecycle in Chapter 3). Talk to your manager about strategic projects you might be able to get involved in. This will help you to start shifting your mindset and developing your strategy skills.

The critical role of the HR Business Partner

HR Business Partner (HRBP): An HR professional who acts as a strategic link between the HR function and the business, bridging the gap between HR strategy and organizational goals.

In an article published in 2018 entitled 'The Critical Importance of the HR Business Partner', McKinsey emphasized the need to evolve the traditional HRBP role into a more strategic and value-driven one, which should be reframed as a 'Talent Value Leader'.[1] The recommendation was based on a survey of global CEOs, which revealed widespread concerns about HR's ability to manage talent strategically. Nearly a decade later, little has changed – HR still struggles to implement talent practices that deliver measurable business value. It's something you might hear often from business leadership: 'HR just doesn't add value, it isn't strategic.'

So what does this mean for you, as someone at the beginning of your career in HR? It is never too early to start thinking with a strategic mindset. The transition to Talent Value Leaders from HR Business Partners requires a focused effort to shift mindsets and build capabilities in both HR and business leaders. This book will help you start thinking this way and show you how to build your capability. It will help you understand where your TA work fits in the overall business strategy, and how your day-to-day work impacts business goals.

Reframing TA

When TA is done well, it's not just about filling roles, it's about attracting, engaging, and enabling talent to drive business performance. Therefore, TA is a strategic growth lever as it helps to shape organizational capability, fuels innovation, and builds future workforce readiness.

In Chapter 1, we looked at how TA has evolved. As a reminder, the term 'talent acquisition' emerged in the early 2000s as businesses began to shift away from transactional hiring (recruitment) and toward a more strategic and value-driven approach. Unlike traditional recruitment, TA embraced longer-term thinking, incorporating workforce planning, employer branding, and candidate experience (covered in Chapters 4, 5 and 6).

By the mid-to-late 2000s, the term was universally adopted, especially in industries facing critical skills shortages. The rise of digital hiring platforms, such as LinkedIn (2003), Indeed (2004), and Glassdoor (2007), has accelerated this evolution today by enabling proactive sourcing and candidate engagement at scale across the globe.

Today, we are witnessing another major shift. As AI and automation streamline routine recruitment tasks, TA is finally freed up to focus on strategic impact – from workforce design, talent intelligence, to brand-building and future skills planning. In some organizations, TA is morphing into simply 'Talent' – a more holistic, integrated function that sits at the heart of business performance.

This evolution is starting to reflect a deeper truth; in a world where products can be easily imitated and technology becomes outdated overnight, it is recognized that people are the key market differentiator driving competitive advantage. TA isn't just about hiring, it's about building 'human capital', which is the skills, knowledge, and experience that strengthen a business. We consider this more in Chapter 8. Strategic talent leaders speak this language of human capital value, not vacancies. They talk about the TA value chain and partner with the business to shape capability, unlock growth and drive innovation.

> **Human capital:** The skills, knowledge and experience that strengthens a business.

> **TA value chain:** The end-to-end process and strategic activities involved in identifying, attracting, selecting and onboarding talent to meet an organization's current and future needs. It frames TA as a strategic business function, not just a hiring task.

Why does investing in people matter?

Organizations that invest in their people consistently outperform their competitors. Skype is a good example. Once a dominant video communications platform, it lost ground to more agile competitors because it failed to innovate through its people. Organizations that prioritize workforce development are more resilient, adaptable and equipped for long-term success.

After studying 1,800 companies, McKinsey identified a group of high-performing organizations – People + Performance (P+P) Winners – that stood out for their ability to attract and grow exceptional talent and deliver top-tier financial results. These P+P Winners had two key strengths:

1 They hire and develop high-performing talent through training, career progression, and development.
2 They consistently outperform competitors on financial measures like revenue growth and profitability.[2]

TA sits at the centre of this strategy. It's no longer just about getting people through the door, it's much more about ensuring every hiring decision supports the broader goals of the organization and fuels future business performance.

Forward-looking companies are already embedding TA into business planning cycles, using technology and insight and leveraging data to drive smarter workforce decisions and long-term value creation.

What does this mean for you?

You are entering TA at an exciting time. Whether you are in a TA team or HR supporting TA, you are likely to have opportunities that your predecessors might not have had. We're at an exciting crossroads, where the most successful TA and HR professionals will evolve from tacticians to strategic business partners – using insight and experience to guide the business, not just support it. By absorbing the advice in this book, you will be ready to grasp these opportunities when they arise, and understand what it takes to elevate your role into a strategic business partner. So much of this comes down to the strength and quality of your relationships with key stakeholders, which we consider later in the chapter.

TA maturity through a hiring manager lens

All too often, outdated mindsets persist across TA, driven by relentless hiring pressures to deliver, overstretched teams, and short-term needs and metrics. Legacy thinking – especially among leaders shaped by pre-2000s recruitment models – reinforces a narrow, reactive view of hiring, reducing TA to a transactional and operational function rather than recognizing it as a strategic enabler of business success.

As one of the few external-facing HR functions, TA is uniquely exposed to market volatility and economic sensitivity. During downturns, the focus often reverts to cost containment and immediate headcount needs, while in periods of business hypergrowth, TA regains strategic prominence, powering employer branding, talent sourcing, and long-term workforce strategies. These ever-shifting conditions of growth and contraction often prevent TA from fully stepping into its strategic potential. It's also a frustrating place to be and can become demotivating for those working in TA.

The recurring boom and bust economic cycle, where TA is deprioritized during downturns and elevated during hypergrowth, reinforces the outdated view that recruitment is simply a transactional process focused solely on filling immediate vacancies.

Your organization's talent maturity is most clearly felt through the strength and quality of your hiring manager relationships. Does a hiring manager simply hand you a job description and ask you to fill a role, or are they open to collaborating with you and working together to determine hiring needs? Figure 2.1 visualizes TA maturity through a hiring manager lens.

FIGURE 2.1 TA maturity through a hiring manager lens

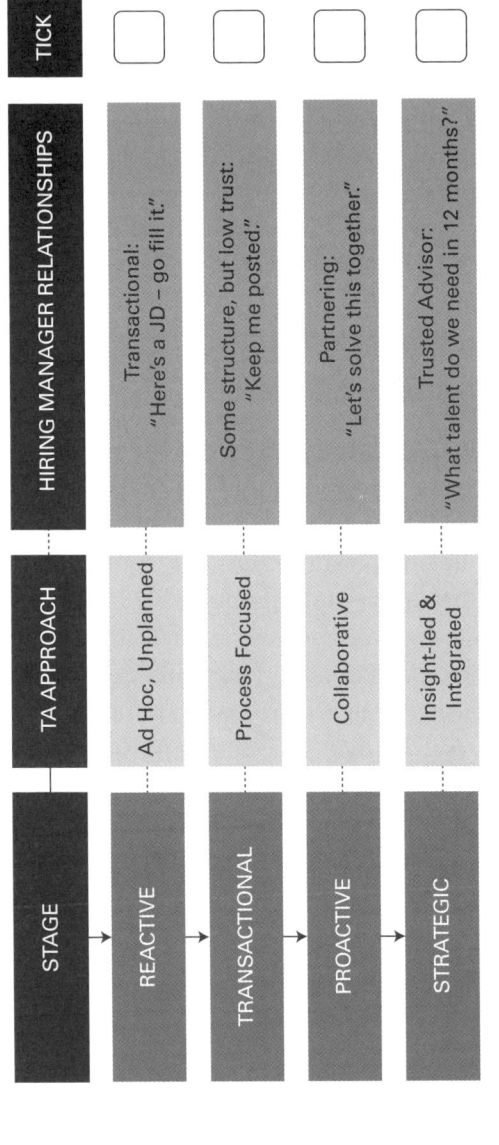

STAGE	TA APPROACH	HIRING MANAGER RELATIONSHIPS	TICK
REACTIVE	Ad Hoc, Unplanned	Transactional: "Here's a JD – go fill it."	
TRANSACTIONAL	Process Focused	Some structure, but low trust: "Keep me posted."	
PROACTIVE	Collaborative	Partnering: "Let's solve this together."	
STRATEGIC	Insight-led & Integrated	Trusted Advisor: "What talent do we need in 12 months?"	

STOP AND THINK

To help you understand your own organization's talent maturity, think about a time when you have worked with a hiring manager. How would you describe the experience, according to the model in Figure 2.1?

Were you expected to operate reactively and deliver solely operational support, or did you partner with the hiring manager to think more strategically about what talent was required?

If you've ticked a more reactive or operational stage, you're not alone. Many TA teams sit here, but recognizing this is the first, crucial step.

Increasing talent maturity

Thankfully, TA maturity isn't fixed – it can most certainly shift, with the right intent and actions. As an early career professional, your influence may be limited, depending on your role and the size of your organization. But look to your TA and executive leaders. How do they talk about talent? If you feel your function is currently reactive and operational, is there any evidence of that changing? Many TA functions are slowly evolving into high-value, high-impact drivers of business success. Don't be scared to ask the right questions, and start to build trust with key stakeholders, such as hiring managers, to demonstrate the potential of TA. We consider talent maturity further, and beyond the hiring manager lens, in Chapter 3.

TOP TIP
Find the right hiring managers

Pick one or two hiring managers open to change. Start to build trust. Use data and talk in terms of business impact, elevating the conversation away from vacancies and CVs to capability, workforce planning and business value. Start to show how TA and HR can drive performance, shape capability, and create future readiness.

Managing conversations with stakeholders

We've talked about how TA can get stuck in transactional work, constantly delivering reports and servicing requests from the business. In this section, we consider this problem in more depth and how, as an early career professional, you can help highlight the issue and, with the support of your manager, push back on requests that deliver little business value.

One of the most important things you can do as an early career professional in TA is get comfortable with data. Jenn Candee, global TA management consultant (former Global TA Executive at Cargill, Mondelez, and SABMiller), says: 'Talent Acquisition holds one of the most powerful assets in any organization: data. With over 6 million insights captured across the entire candidate journey, TA is uniquely positioned as the critical bridge between business objectives and people value.' But data alone doesn't change anything – it's how you tell a story using the data that counts. It's easy to get bogged down in dashboards and reporting cycles in TA, endlessly churning out reports that offer little real value, and have no clear purpose or outcome. The truth is, the business will always 'love' data, but without insight, it's just noise. To break this cycle, we've got to treat data as a tool of influence, not just information. It should help us guide hiring managers, challenge assumptions, and shape smarter decisions.

EXAMPLE

An early careers hiring function receives hundreds of requests from hiring managers for diversity pipeline reports every week, indicating a lack of trust in the recruitment process. The team is bogged down in this cycle of transactional work that offers little real value and does not directly fill roles.

The team leader is aware of the issue and sets out an action plan to free up the team to focus on strategic work while transforming the approach to reporting:

1   Audit the existing reporting.

2   Hold workshops to understand the business's real needs and align on the reports that truly matter.

3   Pause non-essential reports: challenge the team to ask, 'What decisions do these reports help us make?' and focus on value-driven insights and action-based recruitment strategies.

This kind of transformation takes time, but ultimately allows teams to focus on high-impact, value-driving activities.

Learning how to say no

In the boxed example, the team leader must push back on business requests to free up their team. The trickiest change to implement is likely to be step three: pausing non-essential reports. To do this, the whole TA team must be challenged to ask, 'What decisions do these reports help us make?' which might involve pushing back on requests from the business. Kinsey Li, data analytics leader and author, says: 'Challenging ad hoc reporting is essential to enabling truly strategic, intelligent operations. This is where you step back, reassess the core business problems and leverage recruitment data to drive smarter, evidence-based decisions.'

To become the kind of Talent Value Leader McKinsey talks about in its article 'The Critical Importance of the HR Business Partner', HR professionals must avoid being pulled into the weeds of transactional and operational issues, and say 'no' occasionally. To become a Talent Value Leader, you will need to get used to pushing different perspectives and seeking to influence others in the business.

TOP TIP
Become a hedgehog

To shift your mindset away from being an order-taker, grow a few prickles. Rather than defaulting to 'yes' every time a hiring manager asks for a report, pause and consider the following two questions:

1 Will this data drive meaningful insight, and help a decision get made?

2 Will this support seasonal hiring goals, or could my time be better spent proactively making hires happen?

Saying 'no' to people in the business, especially when you are early in your career, can feel difficult. Try these tips:

- Start with curiosity, not conflict
  - Ask: 'I'm curious about your request, what decision are you trying to make with this?', or 'What's the urgency or impact?'

- Reframe the no
  - Try: 'We offer standard business reports, and here is what I can offer that will have more impact...'

- Anchor in outcomes, not effort
  - Say: 'Right now, I am focusing on actions that directly contribute to hires, let's revisit this report once we've hit X.'

- Be clear, kind and consistent
  - Reaffirm: 'If you share your specific request in writing, along with why you need this report, I'll feed it into our next data review.'

The process of managing a courageous conversation isn't about being difficult with your stakeholders, it's about maintaining professionalism while taking control back.

Just as our stakeholders expertly learn to manage their own work priorities, TA professionals must also set clear, intentional boundaries. Saying 'no', or even 'not right now' is an integral part of being a strategic partner, not a real-time service desk. The best TA professionals don't churn out reports for the sake of it; instead, they:

- Use tactical questioning to elevate conversations
- Follow clear data strategies, e.g. automating routine data requests, and interpreting, translating, and guiding action

- Bring external insight to inform, educate and help the business calibrate expectations.

This is what it means to move beyond transactional recruiting. It's not just about filling roles – it's about reshaping business thinking.

So, we've successfully learned how to push back on ad hoc reports, but now the focus is on influencing the business and adding real value.

Gaining stakeholders' trust

A key part of our role in TA is to help the business understand the real hiring issues at play. This often comes down to explaining the availability of external talent and connecting it to internal trends so that the organization can respond to real market challenges with clarity and context.

Data alone isn't enough. It's context and analysis that help you to reach insight and make it meaningful. Without insight, data remains just numbers on a page. For instance, if data shows low application rates, insight into market trends can provide a deeper understanding: Is it just the company's issue, or is there a broader industry challenge at play? If candidates aren't hitting your assessment quality benchmarks, it's not always just a process issue – it could point to something more significant, like a branding problem or negative market perception (Chapter 5 considers employer branding). By interpreting data in this way, you can focus on what's driving the challenge and give the business the context it needs to make informed decisions.

Even the best recruitment process can't overcome a perception problem, and you can't expect the same process to work harder when application volumes are down. Using insight to reframe the conversation and focus on what's really driving the challenge will help channel recruitment efforts where they'll have the biggest impact.

Skills for a modern TA and HR mindset

Moving from being just a data processor to becoming a true strategic talent partner requires more than just technical knowledge and expertise. It needs a total mindset shift. Technical skills can be trained, but a mindset shift takes intentionality, self-awareness and a genuine desire to grow. It requires strengths in curiosity and embracing a proactive approach to problem-solving. These core skills influence how we think, act, and approach every challenge. Figure 2.2 shows a taxonomy of skills for modern TA.

Core strengths like data fluency, having a global mindset, digital agility, commercial awareness, and creativity sit at the bottom of the pyramid because they are foundational strengths that represent the knowledge needed to drive meaningful change to transform yourself into a true talent value partner. We consider these strengths in depth in this book's Conclusion, but for now let's take data fluency, global mindset and commercial awareness as three examples:

1 **Data fluency**
   As we've seen, this is not just about reading reports, but interpreting and translating data into actionable insights. In a recruitment intake meeting, for example, you could use external market competitor insights and time-to-hire data to set realistic expectations with hiring managers.
2 **Global mindset**
   This skill helps you navigate cross-regional recruitment challenges. When hiring across different geographies, a global mindset enables recruiters to adapt strategies to regional trends and labour market dynamics, ensuring recruitment approaches are tailored to each market's needs. For instance, in a recruitment update meeting, you might highlight talent shortages in a specific location and guide the business toward investing in a longer-term graduate hiring strategy to address the issue.

FIGURE 2.2 A taxonomy of skills for TA

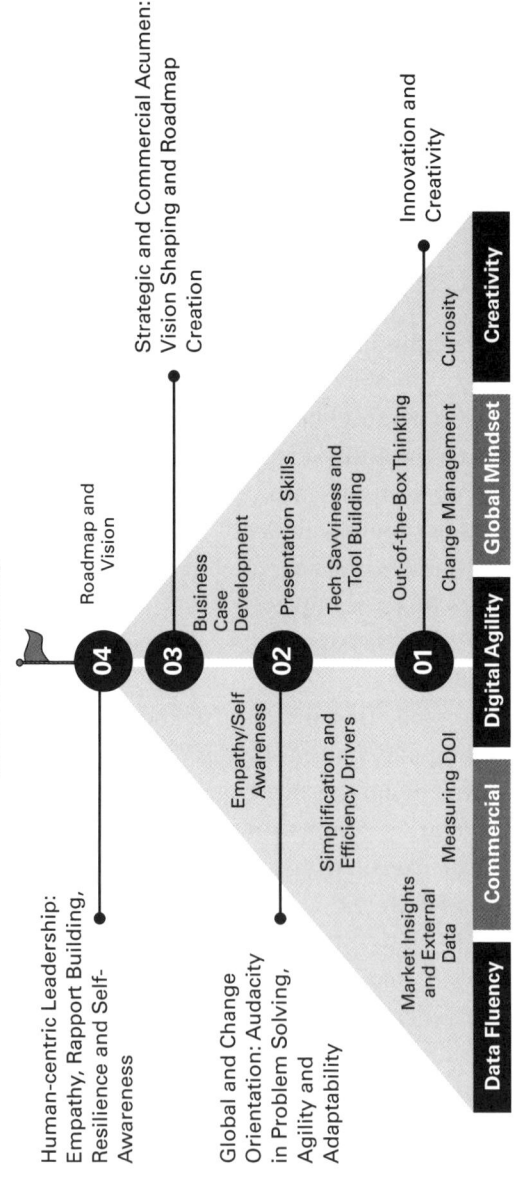

3 **Commercial awareness**
   This skill empowers talent acquisition professionals to align hiring strategies with broader business goals. By understanding the financial drivers of the organization, recruiters can prioritize roles based on ROI, workforce planning needs and market opportunities. For example, you might identify that high agency spend in a particular business unit stems from poor recruitment forecasting and a lack of internal pipelining. You then partner with the business to shift focus to an internal talent pool and proactive sourcing, reducing spend while improving time-to-hire and quality-of-hire.

By embedding some of these core strengths into our daily work, we can develop advanced skills like innovation, vision-setting, business case development, and change management, which appear further up the pyramid. These actionable skills help us execute the strategic mindset that defines a true TA partner.

The taxonomy of skills is quite advanced, so let's look at its practical application, with a couple of basic examples: a recruitment intake meeting and a recruitment update meeting.

Recruitment intake meeting

Skill requirement: Business acumen, communication and problem-solving

- Position yourself as a problem-solver, not a processor.
- Use intake meetings to understand business drivers, not just job specs.
  - Ask the right questions: 'Why now?' 'What's at risk if we don't hire?' and 'How will success be measured?'
  - Align with the business on what great talent looks like.

Skill requirement: Data fluency

- Identify the real business challenges, not just technical aspects.
  - Understand the bigger business context; align hiring strategy to address current talent challenges (e.g. internal mobility, retention).

- Uncover underlying issues.
  - Ask: 'What is your biggest talent challenge right now, and how can TA support you in the next 12 months?'

Recruitment update meeting

Skill requirement: Data fluency, strategic thinking, communication

- Position yourself as a strategic partner by translating data into insights.
- Share meaningful data with insights and not just metrics:
  - Time-to-hire trends: How long is it taking to fill roles compared to market standards?
  - Market brand ranking and Glassdoor insights: How does the company's reputation affect application rates?
  - DE&I insights: Break down drop-off rates by demographic to identify where underrepresented groups may be declining disproportionately at key stages of the recruitment process, e.g. online tests or interview.

Essentially your role is about educating and recalibrating business expectations with evidence – not emotion. It's about using data and insights to guide decision-making and set realistic goals. Beyond simply filling positions, you can add value by consulting on things like retention strategies, internal mobility, and workforce planning.

The key is to first understand the business problem you're solving, rather than simply gathering data for data's sake. It's about focusing on actionable insights that drive strategic solutions, not just numbers on a page.

Metrics that matter

When using data to influence hiring managers, not just inform, there are some must-have metrics to be aware of. Whether you are supporting recruitment or responsible for recruitment itself, these metrics are a mirror into the candidate experience, brand and process, all of which we consider in later chapters of this book. Used correctly, they can provide important indicators to help HR and TA isolate root causes and guide hiring managers on best practices:

CV to hire ratio

This metric can be used to understand:

- Quality of sourcing (refer to Chapter 6).
- Hiring manager confidence.
- Process efficiency.
- Candidate experience.
- Time and cost saving.

Interview to offer ratio

This metric can be used to understand:

- Effectiveness of screening and selection (refer to Chapter 7).
- Hiring manager alignment (expectations).
- Candidate quality.
- Interview experience and process design.

Offer decline reasons (especially related to manager interactions)

This metric can be used to understand:

- EVP challenge (refer to Chapter 5).
- Taking too long – process length inefficiency.
- Candidate experience gaps.

Hiring velocity by team or function

This metric can be used to understand:

- Bottlenecks in the process.
- TA team efficiency.
- Manager engagement.

Candidate satisfaction score (NPS or qualitative)

This metric can be used to understand:

- Perception of employer brand (refer to Chapter 5).
- Experience across the recruitment journey (refer to Chapter 5).
- Drop of risk in the funnel.
- Inclusive experience signals.
- Reasonable adjustments/inclusive process.

WHAT WOULD YOU DO?
Number 2

Background

In businesses with a strong analytical or commercial focus, HR and TA teams often face the challenge of presenting data that can be easily trusted and used to drive decisions. Establishing a single, reliable source of truth is essential to avoid confusion and build trust across teams.

The situation

A global technology firm is insisting that the recruitment team attend more career fairs, believing the weak employer brand is affecting application quality. However, at the business's request, the team has already attended over 100 career fairs in locations misaligned with current hiring location needs. Despite high applicant numbers, a large proportion of candidates are rejected at the initial screening and interview stages, revealing a poor events and outreach strategy and a mismatch between the talent pool and the company's actual needs.

TA has flagged the real issue: a slow, fragmented hiring process – long hiring cycles, slow CV feedback, and lengthy panel interviews (sometimes three or four stages). They propose streamlining feedback loops, reducing interviews to two stages and focusing outreach effort on strategic locations.

Despite this, the business dismisses the data and insists the issue is still on brand visibility.

What would you do? Answer according to your role, whether you are in HR supporting TA, or in TA itself.

Elevating the hiring manager experience

So far in this chapter, we've discussed managing stakeholders day-to-day with ad hoc requests and leveraging data and insights in a meaningful way. But how do we truly deliver value and create an exceptional experience for our key customers: the hiring managers?

The experience that hiring managers desire cannot be easily categorized, as each one has distinct needs. Some may be more strategic, focusing on future products and long-term goals, while others may be more immediate and urgent, requiring fast solutions for current projects. However, the common thread is that hiring managers want the recruitment team to listen to their needs and understand their unique requirements.

Although recruiters and hiring managers share the same ultimate goal – making a successful hire – the path to success and a great hiring manager experience lies in great collaboration. By aligning on expectations and approach, TA, HR and hiring managers can work together more effectively to achieve the desired outcome.

A positive hiring manager experience makes for smoother processes, more informed decisions, and ultimately, stronger hires. By fostering a partnership built on clear communication and alignment, we not only meet hiring managers' needs but also elevate the entire recruitment process. The following are seven guiding principles for greater hiring manager collaboration:

1   Build a culture of insight and influence – use data, expertise and storytelling to guide decisions.

2 Get the foundations right – know the role inside out and set up a recruitment kick-off meeting to align on expectations, timelines and responsibilities.

3 Shift the focus – frame hiring as decision-making, not CV sifting.

4 Incorporate feedback loops – use structured reviews to continuously improve together and collaborate.

5 Deliver proactive, tailored support – offer personal support in activities like strategic sourcing, market mapping and coaching.

6 Elevate conversations and challenge – address key delivery risks early and offer solutions.

7 Ensure regular touchpoints – prepare stakeholders for what's next, e.g. preparing interviewers.

TOP TIP
Start as you mean to go on

A strong recruitment kick-off meeting is essential at the outset of any hiring process. Focus on the following:

- Create a clear, realistic, and collaborative delivery timeline

- Outline the complexity of the role, anticipated market challenges, and internal talent benchmarks.

- Align on hiring manager expectations, clearly defining the must-haves versus the nice-to-haves and identifying what great looks like from a cultural fit perspective.

- Develop a clear, realistic and collaborative delivery timeline from the outset.

This meeting ensures that every hiring manager understands their role and responsibilities throughout the process.

CHAPTER SUMMARY

- TA today isn't just about filling roles, it's about shaping business performance and building human capital that powers long-term success.

- Organizations are at different levels of talent maturity. The relationship between TA and hiring managers provides a window for understanding a business's level of maturity.

- HR and TA professionals must develop the right mindset and capability to elevate conversations with stakeholders from transactional to strategic – using data fluency, a global mindset, business acumen and digital agility to influence the business.

- The two biggest challenges facing HR and TA professionals today are mindset and capability. Developing curiosity, creativity, commercial thinking and digital fluency is essential – they're the skills that underpin more advanced competencies like strategic influence, innovation and change leadership.

- There isn't a single type of hiring manager, but by developing the right skills and mindset, you can start to have more robust conversations that deliver real value and delight your key customers.

- Having the courage to say no will move you from a service desk to a strategic business partner in future.

REVIEW QUESTIONS

1 What are the five key strengths that you need to help you on your journey to become a true strategic talent partner?

2 Describe the four stages of the TA maturity model and the typically aligned TA approach for each stage.

3 Describe three of the five TA metrics that matter.

Endnotes

1 McKinsey (2018) The critical importance of the HR business partner, https://www.mckinsey.com/capabilities/people-and-organizational-performance/our-insights/the-organization-blog/the-critical-importance-of-the-hr-business-partner (archived at https://perma.cc/85B4-RWSK)

2 Madgavkar, A et al (2023) Performance through people: Transforming human capital into competitive advantage, https://www.mckinsey.com/mgi/our-research/performance-through-people-transforming-human-capital-into-competitive-advantage (archived at https://perma.cc/L5GQ-ANV5)

CHAPTER THREE

The foundations of talent acquisition

Introduction

This chapter introduces the fundamental elements of TA. First, we look at the brain and engine behind TA, the '12 building blocks of TA'. These are the key components of a modern TA function, from strategy and vision to the operational muscle and relationship-building needed to make effective hiring happen. We take a deep dive into TA strategy, and demonstrate how a well-crafted one can ensure that TA helps an organization achieve its long-term vision. Next, we look at the TA lifecycle, which outlines the key operational stages a candidate moves through in the hiring process. These five stages align with the five functional TA activity building blocks and underpin the structure for the rest of this book. We end the chapter by looking at the metrics that help you see if a TA strategy is working, and how to evaluate TA maturity levels within your own organization.

> **LEARNING OBJECTIVES**
>
> By the end of this chapter, you will be able to:
> - Understand the key building blocks of TA.
> - Explain how TA fits into business strategy and the importance of an integrated approach to TA.

- Describe the TA lifecycle and how it differs from the TA building blocks.
- Explain how to measure TA success effectively.
- Evaluate TA maturity levels, including within your own organization.
- Understand how the TA building blocks might evolve with AI.

The 12 building blocks of TA

The 12 building blocks of TA serve as foundational components that form the backbone of an effective TA strategy, ensuring that recruitment processes are strategic, sustainable and aligned with business goals. By understanding these core elements of TA, organizations can build a robust and scalable TA function that attracts, engages, and retains top talent. Figure 3.1 shows how the 12 building blocks can be grouped into four main areas:

1 Vision and purpose – the overarching vision, direction, and objectives of the function and how they align with business goals and the future workforce. TA strategy translates this vision into clear priorities, hiring goals, and a roadmap for action.

2 Functional TA activities – focuses on the specialisms within TA, including:

- Workforce planning and recruitment forecasting.
- Employer branding.
- Candidate attraction and sourcing.
- Assessment and selection.
- Onboarding and retention.

Many of these are elements of the TA lifecycle, discussed later in this chapter.

3 TA infrastructure – encompasses the enablement aspects of TA, such as people (skills and abilities), technology, and processes.

4 TA management and oversight – relates to governance, cadence, and systems used to track, measure, and oversee TA activities, including Data and Reporting, Supply Chain Management, and Stakeholder Management.

Smaller businesses may not have a separate TA function, and may combine TA and HR responsibilities, but they can still apply TA best practices and reach a higher level of talent acquisition maturity.

The 'brain' of TA encompasses the strategic elements that guide the function. They inform decision making and optimize strategy. Think of it like a GPS for the TA strategy. These are:

- The vision and strategy.
- Employer branding and employee value proposition.
- Workforce planning.
- Data, insights, and technology.

These building blocks set the direction for how TA aligns with business goals, attracts top talent, and continuously improves.

The 'engine' of TA is where recruiters, coordinators, systems, and processes carry out the actual work and is focused on operational excellence. This includes candidate attraction, sourcing, assessment and selection, hiring manager and stakeholder management, and operations, compliance, and governance. These elements bring the strategy to life, ensuring a seamless, efficient, and compliant recruitment process.

In TA, both the brain and the engine matter – strategy without execution goes nowhere, and execution without strategy leads nowhere.

Why do these building blocks matter to HR?

These building blocks provide a structured framework for a holistic approach to recruitment. This ensures that all TA activities are aligned with the organization's broader goals, driving

FIGURE 3.1 The 12 building blocks of TA

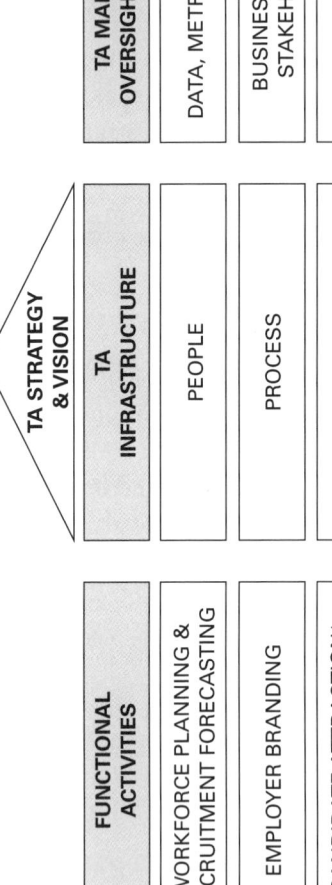

TA STRATEGY & VISION

FUNCTIONAL ACTIVITIES	TA INFRASTRUCTURE	TA MANAGEMENT & OVERSIGHT/GOVERNANCE
WORKFORCE PLANNING & RECRUITMENT FORECASTING	PEOPLE	DATA, METRICS & REPORTING
EMPLOYER BRANDING	PROCESS	BUSINESS PARTNERING/ STAKEHOLDER MGMT
CANDIDATE ATTRACTION/ SOURCING	ENABLING TECHNOLOGY	SUPPLY CHAIN/PARTNERS
ASSESSMENT & SELECTION		
ONBOARDING & RETENTION		

TA BUILDING BLOCKS

strategic growth or fostering a cohesive, high-performing workforce.

If you are working in HR supporting TA rather than within a TA team, a deep technical understanding of these building blocks isn't necessary. However, having a high-level understanding of these pillars and how they work can help you become a more impactful and forward-thinking HR Business Partner.

You'll be able to use this knowledge to drive strategic business discussions and ensure all recruitment efforts are aligned with long-term organizational goals. As an HR professional, your main priority is to align the company's people strategy with its overall business goals and help address any people gaps that might be stopping the business from achieving its objectives.

By focusing on getting the right people in the door from the start, you're setting the right foundation for future growth and reducing the risk of people-related challenges down the line, or downstream.

A key part of your role is helping the company to connect with this mindset, understand and embrace the idea that recruitment matters and the people hired now are crucial to long-term success. Encouraging stakeholders to foster a strategic collaboration with TA will ensure that all recruitment efforts are seamlessly aligned with the company's long-term vision.

By gaining a broader understanding of how the TA building blocks go beyond execution, you'll position yourself as a trusted business partner, build business credibility and strengthen your capability to have meaningful conversations with the business. This will empower you to help shape a cohesive, future-ready workforce strategy that drives organizational growth and sustainability.

The five core functional activities

Let's now turn to the five core functional activities, or building blocks, that a TA function delivers. These are shown on the left of Figure 3.1. These five essential disciplines represent the core of TA execution. In other words, they are 'what' a TA function executes to drive the effectiveness and outcomes of recruitment strategies. They align with the TA lifecycle, which we explore later in this chapter:

1   Workforce Planning and Recruitment Forecasting.
2   Employer Branding and Attraction.
3   Sourcing and Candidate Engagement.
4   Assessment and Selection.
5   Onboarding and Retention Strategy.

The additional building blocks shown in Figure 3.1 focus more on the 'how' of TA and are related to TA enablement. For example, technology and data are key enablers of the hiring process, resulting in faster and smoother recruitment and enhancing the overall candidate experience. These building blocks support the organization's ability to grow and adapt in a changing digital landscape.

WHAT WOULD YOU DO?
Number 3

Imagine you're the HRBP in a fast-growing global organization facing the following familiar and complex challenge.

Despite investing in new sales roles and recruitment, the company continues to miss its sales targets and performance goals.

The business is shifting to a digital future to stay competitive, with a new Enterprise Resource Planning (ERP) system and Applicant Tracking System (ATS), and now, it must identify talent with the right digital skills to support the ongoing business transformation and foster a more collaborative and accountable culture.

TA has been tasked with hiring the right people to support the digital shift, but needs to ensure these candidates fit into the evolving culture and possess a global mindset.

Key issues at a glance:

- The company relies on outdated, manual processes with regional silos – sales performance is tracked manually.
- The workforce needs modern digital and collaborative skills.
- TA must hire sales professionals that are aligned with the business's growth needs and shifting culture.
- The current workforce is not operating in a global team, with duplication and a lack of transparency resulting in missed client opportunities.
- Recruitment is viewed as a reactive function, and the business is expecting a more proactive service to identify talent from its competitors.
- A global review of recruitment demonstrated a lack of standardization across TA. In particular, inconsistent employer brands, role profiles and assessment frameworks.

Your role as a strategic HRBP

This scenario is common and difficult. TA teams are often expected to deliver results without the context, insight, or strategic visibility needed to identify and attract the right quality of talent. As an HR Business Partner, you're in a unique position to bridge this gap. You have the clearest view of the business strategy, its people challenges, and what's needed to support growth. As you are an enabler of business strategy, take a moment to reflect on how you might be able to support your TA colleagues.

TA strategy and vision

TA strategy and vision is the top TA building block shown in Figure 3.1. In Chapter 1, we looked at how TA is fundamentally about identifying, attracting, and hiring skilled talent to meet an organization's needs. A TA strategy takes this a step further. It is a comprehensive plan that helps optimize how an organization sources, recruits, and retains talent.

> **TA strategy:** A comprehensive plan that helps optimize how an organization sources, recruits, and retains talent.

A well-crafted TA strategy ensures that the key elements of TA and related processes align with the company's long-term vision. It encompasses a holistic approach to talent management and links organizational needs to nurturing relationships with potential candidates and future hires.

As your role evolves, you will be in a unique position to support TA and advocate for a proactive, long-term strategy that supports and enhances TA's recruitment recommendations.

THE POWER OF AN INTEGRATED APPROACH

A good strategy includes a series of interconnected processes and initiatives designed to align the organization's talent needs with its future business objectives. It goes beyond just filling open roles, and addresses the broader challenges, such as societal, technological, or economic shifts, that can hinder the organization's ability to attract, engage, and retain the talent needed for future success (refer to Chapter 1).

A successful strategy should consider the evolving needs of the business and identify the core skills necessary for growth. It should also focus on developing a workforce that fosters innovation to maintain the organization's competitive edge.

It helps the company stay ahead by focusing not just on attracting talent, but on employee retention, supporting long-term development, and championing diversity and inclusion. A great strategy also strengthens an employer brand, creating candidate experiences that stand out in a candidate-driven market. At the same time, it should also allow the organization to continually adapt to external changes, industry trends and evolving candidate preferences. It ensures that all TA efforts remain resilient and competitive with the talent needed to reach its long-term goals.

The earlier 'What would you do?' feature demonstrates the lynchpin role TA plays in developing a coherent strategy that aligns hiring with the organization's long-term digital ambitions. Talent acquisition needs to take more of a proactive stance to help the business stay ahead and develop solutions that draw on all the key TA building blocks to find people with the right skills for the future.

This is relevant to you even if you are in a pure HR role, as you may collaborate with TA in shaping these solutions, making sure they align with broader business goals. You're also in a unique position to bring insights on emerging workforce trends, such as an ageing workforce, shifting skills gaps, or evolving employee expectations. Your role might also stretch into strengthening the employer brand to help attract the right talent or support cultural integration as the business grows or enters new markets (we cover this in Chapter 5). In moments such as the one described in the 'What would you do?' feature, your contribution may be less about finding the answers and more about asking the right questions. This is your opportunity to guide the business on a journey, influencing how talent is thought about, not just as a function but as a future-shaping strategy.

STOP AND THINK

Consider your current role.

1 What role can you play in helping TA move from operational to strategic?

2 How can your insight into the business help guide smarter, future-focused hiring decisions?

3 Where do your people challenges intersect with TA's evolving capabilities?

For example, if your organization implements a new ATS or recruitment process, in this moment of change, your contribution is less about finding the answers and more about asking the right questions to reduce business or people risk.

The importance of getting TA strategy right

TA strategy must be carefully planned to address the right business problems. For example, a strategy with a large attraction budget directed towards employer branding may not be effective if it leads to a flood of irrelevant job applications, mismatched and excessive applications from inappropriate locations, or is based on lower recruitment demand. (For more on employer branding, go to Chapter 5.)

In this case, the strategy is misaligned and overly aggressive. If your visibility isn't targeted towards the roles, skills or geographies aligned specifically to hiring demand, then you will end up with a poor candidate experience, and it could be detrimental to your employer brand rather than enhancing it. Candidates may complain about being 'ghosted' or ignored, which can harm the perception of your organization. If they experience a lack of communication, they might view the company negatively as not being an 'employer of choice'. Furthermore, it may lead to criticism of the company's values of 'transparency' and 'equity', as the direct experience of inconsistency between branding efforts and candidate experience could be seen as misleading. This criticism may find itself with bad feedback and reviews on platforms such as Glassdoor, which will in turn become a vicious cycle as the organization would need to use budget and resources to correct these perceptions. This example highlights the importance of getting TA strategy right. To further illustrate this, read the real-world example about Virgin Media's poor candidate experience. It highlights the importance of using data and insights to shape the future talent acquisition strategy and emphasizes that TA and HR professionals must remain curious and use evidence-based information to drive decision-making and any process improvements across the TA lifecycle.

REAL-WORLD EXAMPLE
Virgin Media's poor candidate experience

In TA, we often worry about the consequences of a poor candidate experience. A prominent example of what can go wrong happened at Virgin Media in 2018.

The company implemented an automated recruitment process that sent out impersonal auto-rejection emails to unsuccessful applicants. Candidates enraged by the Virgin's brand promise – *to provide a great customer experience with the best technology* – complained of the lack of authenticity and the impersonal nature of the rejection emails. They felt 'ghosted', or underappreciated, damaging Virgin's glowing reputation for customer service.

The TA strategy was flawed and not aligned with business objectives. It was entirely focused on efficiency drivers, which was at the expense of candidate experience.

Using data and insights from the internal customer retention team, it discovered that almost two-thirds of the regretted candidates were 'detractors' – meaning they would not recommend Virgin Media. To make matters worse, 18 per cent of the unsuccessful candidates were current Virgin Media customers and 6 per cent of them switched to another provider because of the poor experience. The candidate experience didn't just affect recruitment, it was impacting customer retention too. This unfortunate TA strategy cost Virgin Media £4–5 million of revenue per year.

This prompted a completely new TA strategy centred on providing candidates with an exemplary service.[1]

Fortunately, every cloud has a silver lining. Virgin learned from this feedback, and recognized that the effects of their approach extended beyond recruitment. Analysis showed it was ten times more expensive to attract new customers through marketing than to retain those already engaging with the company as applicants.

You should by now have a good understanding of the TA building blocks, from TA vision and strategy, to the functional TA activities, TA infrastructure and TA management and oversight. While the TA building blocks establish the foundation for a strategic TA framework, the TA lifecycle outlines the specific stages and activities candidates go through, from identifying talent needs to fully integrating new hires into the organization. We'll go on to look at that now.

The TA lifecycle: a tactical execution framework

TA lifecycle: The key operational stages and journey a candidate moves through during the hiring process.

The TA lifecycle encapsulates every stage of the journey a candidate moves through during the hiring process. This is more tactical and execution-focused, from planning and attracting the right talent to engaging, sourcing, assessing, and ultimately onboarding candidates. These stages follow a structured approach to ensure recruitment aligns with the organization's talent needs and strategic goals.

The stages of the TA lifecycle

The TA lifecycle represents the key operational stages and journey a candidate moves through during the hiring process. It forms the structure for the rest of this book, as each chapter explores the detailed activities involved in each stage. As shown in Figure 3.2, it consists of five key recruitment workflows that ensure a structured and effective approach to recruitment:

1 Plan: TA starts with strategic workforce planning (WFP). Planning ensures alignment with business needs by defining the required skills, experience and competencies for future objectives (Chapter 4).

2 Attract: Bringing the right talent into the pipeline requires employer branding, compelling job descriptions, and targeted outreach strategies (Chapter 5).

3 Engage/source: Once candidates show interest, this phase focuses on relationship-building, proactive sourcing, and converting interest into applications (Chapter 6).

4 Assess/select: Candidates are evaluated for both technical skills and cultural fit through a structured, fair, and unbiased process (Chapter 7).

5 Onboard: A strong onboarding experience ensures new hires integrate smoothly, reducing turnover and accelerating productivity (Chapter 8).

FIGURE 3.2   The TA lifecycle

The difference between the building blocks and lifecycle

At first glance, the TA building blocks and lifecycle may appear similar, but there is a subtle difference. The TA building blocks provide the strategic foundation for an effective recruitment function. Each block plays a crucial role in shaping a strategic and effective TA process. No single component is more important than the others; they complement each other and work together to build a strong, harmonized recruitment strategy that supports business objectives.

By understanding and applying these building blocks, as an HR professional, you'll be better equipped to:

· Align recruitment efforts with business needs.
· Attract and retain top talent.
· Make better data-driven hiring decisions.
· Support long-term talent development.

While the building blocks provide the foundation for a successful TA strategy, the TA lifecycle focuses on the actual execution and delivery. It outlines the tactical steps for executing the strategy and moving candidates through the hiring process. By mastering both, HR professionals can ensure that TA is not just reactive but a proactive driver of business success.

STOP AND THINK

Reflect on your own organization. How is your TA function structured?

- Would you describe it as basic, with only a few TA building blocks?
- Or is it more mature, with most, or all of the 12 building blocks in place?

Fill out the TA building blocks assessment template shown in Table 3.1 to help you.

Purpose of this exercise

Evaluate how mature and effective your TA function is across all key building blocks.

How to complete the assessment

For each TA Building Block, assess whether practices are:

- 1 = Not in place / ad hoc
- 3 = Partially in place / inconsistently applied
- 5 = Fully in place, scalable and consistent

Write any comments describing:

- Gaps or weaknesses.
- Suggested improvements.

Be as candid as possible, this will drive your action plan.

Scoring

- After rating all 12 building blocks, sum the scores.
- Calculate the average score by dividing the total by 12.

- Use the interpretation guide below to understand your TA maturity.

Average score range	TA maturity level	Interpretation
1.0–1.9	Low	TA is largely reactive and inconsistent. Strong improvements needed across all areas.
2.0–3.4	Developing	Some building blocks are partially in place, but processes are inconsistent and lack scalability.
3.5–5.0	High	Strong evidence of mature, strategic, and consistent TA practices that support organizational goals.

TABLE 3.1   TA building blocks assessment template

Focus	TA building block	In place, scale 1, 3 and 5	Comments (gaps, improvements needed)
Vision	Vision and strategy		
Core functional activities	Strategic WFP		
	Employer branding		
	Talent attraction and sourcing		
	Assessment and selection		
	Onboarding		

TABLE 3.1   *continued*

Focus	TA building block	In place, scale 1, 3 and 5	Comments (gaps, improvements needed)
TA management	Data metrics and reporting		
	Stakeholder management		
	Third-party partners		
TA infrastructure	Technology (ATS, CRM, etc.)		
	People capability		
	Recruitment process consistency		

Once completed, this exercise will give you a clear snapshot of your TA organization's current state and help identify areas for strategic improvement. You may want to return to this exercise after you have worked through the subsequent chapters in this book.

Key TA metrics that define success

In your capacity as an early career HR or TA professional, you might wonder whether the TA strategy you're supporting is actually working. It's a valid business concern. A successful TA strategy should be data-driven and backed by internal and external market insights. Too often, recruitment initiatives fall short because they're poorly implemented, unfocused, or not backed by any real data. A strong TA strategy should be designed around clear metrics, and new initiatives must be measured to ensure they're driving real, successful outcomes that help the organization to support goals like increasing revenue, establishing a new presence in markets or regions, promoting gender diversity, hiring for new digital skills, or securing scarce skills in specific regions.

In many cases, TA tends to rely heavily on a narrow set of traditional recruitment metrics to define success, often centred around quantitative or 'hard' measures. While these metrics have their place, they tend to be very narrow in scope and often miss the broader strategic impact of TA within the business. These traditional measures include:

- Time to hire – measures the speed of filling roles. Long times may indicate inefficiencies or misaligned sourcing.
- Quality of hire – assesses performance of new hires through feedback, productivity and turnover within the first year.
- Candidate experience – gauges candidate satisfaction. Negative feedback can highlight process flaws and employer brand issues.
- Cost per hire – evaluates recruitment spend versus results, identifying inefficiencies like high agency fees.

However, as TA becomes more sophisticated, 'softer', more qualitative measures have emerged. These metrics should not be underestimated and provide a deeper understanding of the TA value chain (the end-to-end process of how value is created through TA). These metrics offer a more nuanced perspective on success and help organizations assess long-term impact beyond just numbers.

TA value chain: A more sophisticated method of measuring the overall effectiveness of recruitment efforts by measuring business success. It refers to how value is created through the TA process.

The TA value chain is a relatively new concept. Companies like Google, Unilever, Accenture, and IBM are leading the way with data-driven recruitment strategies. These companies focus not only on value-driven hiring to ensure cultural fit but also on boosting retention through internal mobility and measuring candidate experience as part of the recruitment process. Enhanced measures that provide an understanding of the TA value chain include:

- Diversity of hire – tracks alignment with diversity goals and the diversity of your talent pool.
- Employer ranking/employer brand – a strong employer brand attracts top candidates and enhances the reach of your targeted audience.
- Candidate retention (post-hiring) – indicates how well hires fit the culture; high turnover suggests misalignment with expectations.
- Sourcing mix – identifies top sourcing channels (e.g. job boards, internal mobility, referrals) and helps refine strategy.
- Offer acceptance rate/withdraw/renege – a low acceptance or high renege rate can indicate issues with eh compensation package or employer brand.
- Talent loss in process – tracks candidates who drop out, signalling potential process issues or unmet expectations.

Even if you do not manage hiring processes directly in your role (if you work in HR, supporting TA instead), understanding the softer, more nuanced metrics that drive value is just as crucial as traditional recruitment metrics. These tend to resonate with the business, and also give a good indicator of whether the TA strategy is valued by stakeholders, and how the business embraces advocacy for the TA strategy. These additional insights will also help you contribute to more strategic discussions and ensure that TA is aligned with the long-term goals of the business.

The TA maturity model in action

Before we dive into the next chapters and explore the elements of the TA lifecycle, let's consider how you can assess and understand the overall impact of your TA function. In Chapter 2, we looked at how to assess your organization's talent maturity through the lens of the hiring managers. That was more to do with TA's current level of influence and how it is perceived within the organization. Here, we'll look at a maturity model which can help you understand the current state of your TA processes and practices across the TA lifecycle, helping you identify areas for improvement.

The TA maturity model provides a structured path to evaluate your organization's recruitment strategies, technologies, processes, and people. It also provides a roadmap for advancing toward more sophisticated, efficient and scalable industry best practices. It's worth noting that the model is continuously evolving, as TA evolves, particularly with AI. A typical TA maturity model includes the following levels:

1 **Initial/Reactive:** Ad hoc, unstructured recruitment processes.
2 **Defined:** More standardized and structured recruitment practices, but TA processes remain limited.
3 **Integrated:** Recruitment efforts are aligned across the TA lifecycle with broader business and HR strategies.
4 **Strategic:** TA becomes a strategic business partner, leveraging data and analytics with advanced technology to align talent needs with organizational goals.
5 **Optimized/Innovative:** TA processes are continuously optimized with cutting-edge technologies, predictive analytics, and proactive talent management strategies.

This five-step pathway to more sophisticated maturity allows organizations to assess and improve their TA function over time and within the context of their own operating or people constraints. From a TA leadership perspective, this model

FIGURE 3.3   TA maturity model

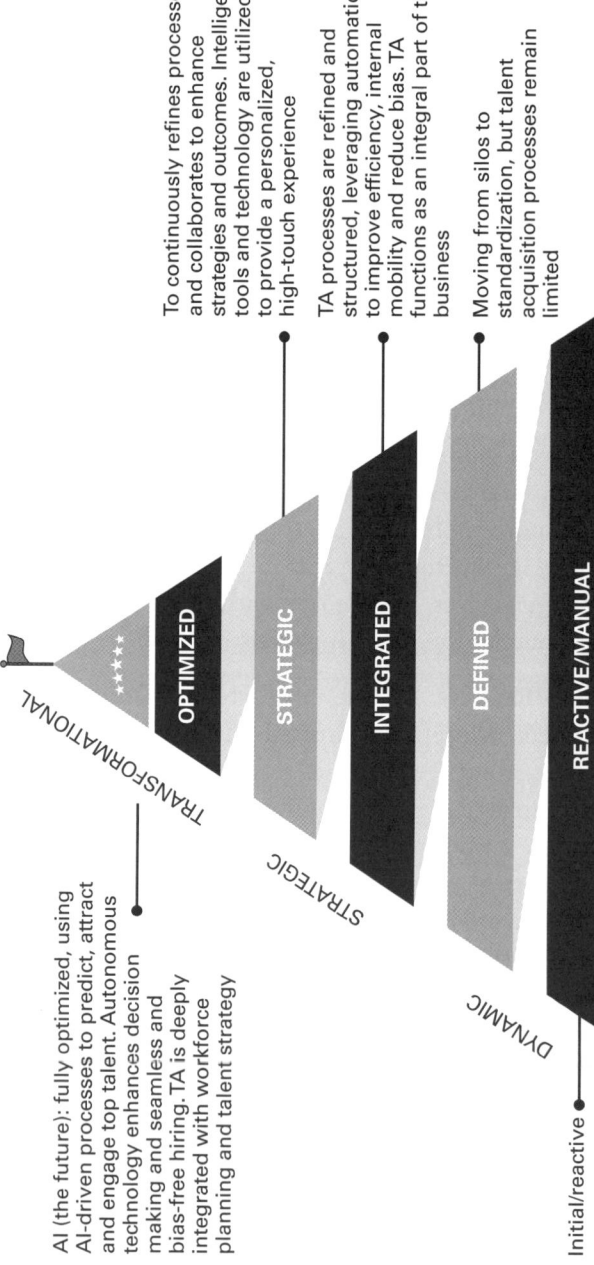

AI (the future): fully optimized, using AI-driven processes to predict, attract and engage top talent. Autonomous technology enhances decision making and seamless and bias-free hiring. TA is deeply integrated with workforce planning and talent strategy

To continuously refines processes and collaborates to enhance strategies and outcomes. Intelligent tools and technology are utilized to provide a personalized, high-touch experience

TA processes are refined and structured, leveraging automation to improve efficiency, internal mobility and reduce bias. TA functions as an integral part of the business

Moving from silos to standardization, but talent acquisition processes remain limited

TRANSFORMATIONAL

OPTIMIZED

STRATEGIC

INTEGRATED

DEFINED

REACTIVE/MANUAL

STRATEGIC

DYNAMIC

Initial/reactive

provides a structured framework to identify gaps and opportunities in the TA function, ensuring alignment with strategic goals. However, for those early in their HR careers, it's less about mastering the model itself and more about understanding how your role supports and contributes to the TA transformation agenda alongside the business.

HOW THE BUILDING BLOCKS MIGHT EVOLVE WITH AI

As mentioned in this book's Introduction, AI is transforming the way TA operates and is beginning to automate many traditional TA tasks. This means that organizations can streamline teams and reallocate resources towards more strategic talent initiatives. This shift may allow TA to focus more on WFP, internal mobility, skills-based hiring, and long-term talent development. In other words, the building blocks may evolve to incorporate talent development and management, rather than just acquisition. TA functions may be reclassified as simply 'Talent'. Some forward-thinking organizations are already making the shift to a more integrated talent management function under HR, blending TA and Talent responsibilities. How widely and quickly this shift happens may depend on an organization's culture, size and the pace of technological adoption. Chapter 8 and the Conclusion cover this in more detail.

STOP AND THINK

Take a moment to reflect on your organization's current approach to balancing technology automation with human connectivity in your talent strategy. Consider the following:

- How is your organization currently navigating this transition toward more automated and AI-driven talent processes?
- What do you see as the key benefits of adopting more automation and AI within TA and HR?

- What are the potential risks or downsides of this shift, especially concerning culture, candidate experience, or decision-making?
- Do you believe that integrating automation and AI will ultimately make HR more effective in driving its people strategies?

WHAT WOULD YOU DO?
Number 4

Your organization is operating at level 1 of the TA maturity model, where recruitment is very manual, inconsistent and reactive. The business is ready for change and seeks more strategic support to enhance the effectiveness and efficiency of its hiring processes.

The hiring managers have asked you to help the team shift from a reactive approach to a more standardized, structured, and proactive TA process that aligns with the organization's growth objectives.

The TA team wants to improve how hiring is done, as right now it is messy and rushed. You've been asked to help make it more organized and consistent. Think of the small changes you could initiate that would make the recruitment process smoother for candidates and hiring managers.

CHAPTER SUMMARY

- The 12 building blocks of a modern TA function can be grouped into four main areas: Vision and Purpose, Functional TA Activities, TA Infrastructure, and TA Management and Oversight. Together, they form the 'brain' and 'engine' of TA.
- TA goes beyond just filling roles, it's a strategic function that drives business success by aligning hiring with long-term goals.
- While the five pillars of the TA lifecycle (Plan, Attract, Engage/ Source, Assess, and Onboard) represent the 'what' of

recruitment execution, additional TA building blocks focus on the 'how', such as enablement and process integration.

- You can measure the success of your recruitment strategies through both traditional and emerging metrics. While classic recruitment metrics like time-to-hire and cost-per-hire are still relevant, organizations must also embrace qualitative indicators, such as candidate experience, cultural fit, internal mobility, and long-term impact, to capture the full value of TA.

- The TA value chain and TA maturity model can be used to improve recruitment from reactive to strategic.

- As AI evolves, TA is merging with talent management, focusing on skills-based hiring, internal development, and predictive analytics. TA is changing rapidly, creating new opportunities for HR professionals.

REVIEW QUESTIONS

1 Can you describe the difference between the TA building blocks and the TA lifecycle?

2 Can you identify and describe the key building blocks that contribute to creating an effective TA strategy?

3 Do you understand how these building blocks contribute to aligning TA strategy with broader organizational goals?

4 Can you evaluate whether the strategy is designed for effective execution in your current or future organizational context?

Endnote

1 Steiner, K (2017) Bad candidate experience cost Virgin Media $5m annually – here is how they turned that around, 15 March, LinkedIn, https://www.linkedin.com/business/talent/blog/talent-acquisition/bad-candidate-experience-cost-virgin-media-5m-annually-and-how-they-turned-that-around (archived at https://perma.cc/BC2Z-NUPS)

CHAPTER FOUR

Workforce planning and recruitment forecasting

Introduction

In this chapter, we dive into one of the most important areas of TA. Workforce planning (WFP) is the true brain of TA. It's the strategic blueprint, the 'thinking cap' that ensures organizations are equipped with the right talent at the right time. It's all about anticipating future needs and mapping out the workforce to align with business goals.

Unfortunately, many businesses treat WFP as an operational function rather than leveraging it as critical driver of long-term business success. This chapter will help you to understand the difference, and assess your own organization to understand how it approaches this critical building block of TA.

We begin by looking at what WFP is and why it's important for organizations. We progress by looking at why it's often difficult for organizations to do it well. We look at the three different types: strategic, operational and tactical (which is most often referred to as recruitment forecasting). Finally, we look at data sources that can be used to inform WFP decisions.

LEARNING OBJECTIVES

By the end of this chapter, you will be able to:

- Understand the importance of WFP and why it's critical for future-proofing talent strategy.
- Recognize the challenges in implementing WFP in practice and how to overcome them.
- Describe the differences between strategic, operational and tactical WFP.
- Explain how to use data to inform WFP decisions.

Why workforce planning matters

Workforce planning: The process of analysing, forecasting and planning workforce supply and demand, assessing gaps and determining targeted talent strategies to ensure the organization has the right people, with the right skills, in the right place at the right time.

Think of WFP as the prefrontal cortex of TA's brain. This part of the brain is where big decisions happen, the strategy is formed, and the future is planned. Just like the prefrontal cortex guides you in making smart, long-term decisions, WFP keeps TA sharp, aligned, and future-focused in meeting the organization's talent needs head-on.

Yet, WFP is so often misunderstood. Similar to the brain itself, it's wildly complicated, always processing information to make decisions and solve problems. WFP requires constant input, working behind the scenes to adjust, adapt, and recalibrate based on ever-changing needs. As such, WFP is one of the most critical components of TA. It sits right at the front of the recruitment process, just like the prefrontal cortex sits right behind the forehead. Despite its importance, WFP is often underdeveloped and overlooked in organizations, lagging behind other aspects of TA in businesses, for reasons we will consider now.

Making workforce planning work for your business

Strategic WFP helps companies align hiring needs with long-term business goals and anticipate future workforce requirements. By having an effective WFP strategy, organizations can predict future talent needs, identify the required skills, assess the current workforce, and address any long-term skills gaps. This process ensures that businesses are equipped with the right people at the right time, supporting the very definition of TA.

The reason WFP can lag behind other aspects of TA is that it often sits outside of TA, in a separate function or team, or even in a standalone role, if the role exists at all.

This dynamic makes it harder to align with immediate recruitment needs. WFP requires a holistic strategic view of the organization's overall goals, which can be difficult to obtain without the right data, tools, or cross-department collaboration. When you factor in decentralized business models and global entities, then the task becomes insurmountable. With multiple teams, regions, and cultural differences involved, aligning workforce needs globally across all levels of the organization requires careful consideration and a comprehensive strategy, making it an even more challenging undertaking.

WFP also requires highly specialized skills – a blend of strategic, analytical and operational skills – and expertise to execute effectively, requiring specific frameworks and processes to be built that allow companies to see where they can better 'build' talent and capabilities within the organization. Typically, industries operating in scarce skills environments, such as engineering, including the military, or with large capital programmes, such as building nuclear power stations over more than ten years, are often more accredited and motivated to do this well. They must carefully plan their workforce to ensure they have the right talent in place throughout long, complex projects like these.

Given its complexity, many organizations choose to retain professional and consulting services firms to review their workforce strategies. This is especially true because WFP involves predicting future needs in a dynamic, externally driven, and nuanced environment, where market trends, economic factors, and industry shifts can all impact workforce requirements.

The three levels of workforce planning

We won't go into detail about WFP methodologies, as it is hugely scientific. It's enough to know that there are three levels: strategic, operational and tactical.

Strategic WFP: A long-term and holistic approach to aligning workforce and future skills and capability needs with business strategy. This process requires analysing, forecasting, and planning for an organization's future workforce needs – typically over a time horizon of 3–5 years or longer.

Operational WFP: A short-term, reactive approach to WFP focusing on day-to-day execution and filling of immediate roles without planning – with a time horizon anywhere from a few months to a year.

Recruitment forecasting/tactical WFP: A mid-term, demand-driven approach to WFP addressing medium-term hiring needs (12 months to three years) and helps predict how many hires will be required with some planning.

Strategic WFP

Strategic WFP can be challenging to implement due to its time-consuming nature, resource intensity, cost, and difficulty in forecasting workforce needs amidst unpredictable external factors and an unknown operating environment. There are six key principles to strategic WFP, often framed around the Buy, Borrow, Bounce, Build, Bind, and Bot model. These principles help organizations determine the best approach to managing their talent needs in a changing landscape:

- Buy: Hiring external talent to fill immediate gaps in the workforce, instead of developing internal talent. Generally used for critical skills roles.
- Borrow: Bringing in external expertise temporarily to bridge skills gaps, for example, contractors or temporary workers.
- Bounce: Describes employee turnover or attrition, where employees leave an organization for better opportunities, personal reasons or retirement.
- Build: Refers to developing talent internally through training, development programmes, and career growth opportunities, i.e. investing in a graduate programme. Used to foster loyalty and long-term employee engagement.
- Bind: Binding employees refers to developing strong employee retention programmes, or offering retention packages for key talent to stay within the organization for key strategic positions.
- Bot: This refers to streamlining activities through technology to reduce staff costs and drive efficiencies. It is the replacement of roles through technology and automation, i.e. AI.
- Blend: A newer and evolving WFP strategy to integrate hybrid and cross-functional teams, typically in tech firms. This combines different types of talent (internal, external, tech) into agile, project-based teams encouraging collaboration across silos or disciplines.

To bring this to life for you as someone early in your career, an organization facing a significant skills gap might do one of two things:

1 Buy temporary talent to fill immediate needs.
2 Take a longer-term approach by building talent through early talent programmes. For critical roles, the organization could focus on binding talent with retention strategies with competitive long-term incentive plans (LTIPs) to minimize risks and ensure key employees stay.

Both TA and HR professionals often find strategic workforce planning difficult, as it can feel overly theoretical and lack direct practicality in day-to-day operations. But failing to do it well can have dire consequences for businesses. The Blockbuster real-world example demonstrates the importance of strategic WFP.

> **Buy, Borrow, Bounce, Build, Bind, and Bot, Blend:** Strategic WFP principles that help organizations decide their best approach to managing talent needs in an ever-changing landscape.

> REAL-WORLD EXAMPLE
> The fall of Blockbuster
>
> In the early 2000s, the world was buzzing with new technology. Broadband speeds were getting faster, enabling the rise of future streaming and digital media. Blockbuster, once the most popular American and global video rental chain, was caught off guard because its strategic WFP was reactive rather than proactive. Instead of planning ahead, leadership failed to recognize the global shift toward online streaming services, and the company was slow to develop the skills and infrastructure needed to compete with new platforms like Netflix.
>
>   By continuing to prioritize its traditional video rental stores, Blockbuster missed the opportunity to pivot to the changing

technological patterns and consumer behaviour, and Netflix's rise left it behind. By the time Blockbuster attempted to embrace digital transformation, it was too late, and the giant collapsed. This case illustrates the dangers of failing to anticipate shifts in the workforce landscape and market disruption. There are many more case studies of poor workforce planning strategies, including General Motors, Sears, Toys R Us and Kodak.[1]

WFP is positioned at the first stage of the TA building blocks (refer to Chapter 3). If that foundation is missing, there's nothing to build upon. Without a clear strategic framework or long-term foresight, TA lacks the necessary guidance for future recruitment planning and is left to react and focus on tactical hiring needs rather than proactively shaping the future workforce.

Even when TA is provided with a comprehensive strategic workforce plan, it can be difficult to execute. These plans are typically too high-level, focused on future skills gaps, and hard to translate into short-term recruitment goals, for the next three to six months or a year. The long-term outlook doesn't always align with the immediate, specific needs of recruitment, making it difficult to bridge the gap between strategic foresight and tactical execution.

KEY POINT

A well-defined strategic workforce plan is crucial for enabling a more proactive approach to recruiting. It helps teams anticipate short-term hiring needs, source more effectively and stay ahead of recruitment challenges.

Operational WFP

Most businesses rely on basic operational WFP, which focuses more on the day-to-day execution of recruitment and filling of immediate roles. Similar to strategic workforce planning, it centres on having the right people in the right place at the right time, but over a short-term horizon – anywhere from a few months to a year – and dealing with immediate staffing needs based on current operational demand. The data is much more easily available to HR and TA, for example:

- Current workforce data
  - Recruitment data
- Headcount
  - Turnover trends, Internal mobility and promotion data
  - Skills inventories, including which ones are held by mostly older employees
- Employee demographics
  - Age profile of current employees
  - Sick leave
  - Scheduled absences (maternity/paternity leave)
- Performance data
  - Internal mobility and promotional data
- Project deadlines
- Real-time workload analysis
  - Seasonal demand

Recruitment forecasting/tactical WFP

Recruitment forecasting is a way of predicting future hiring needs and timelines. It is a more strategic approach than operational WFP and addresses medium-term hiring needs (12 months to three years). It's especially valuable for organizations with high turnover, such as healthcare, technology and manufacturing as well as those with strong success plans or seasonal demand (such as retail staff). It enables HR teams to align staffing levels with future needs.

Recruitment forecasting is straightforward. It requires an understanding of the business's day-to-day operations and workforce needs, as well as the ability to quickly adapt to changing market conditions and business priorities.

Table 4.1 outlines the key differences between strategic WFP and recruitment forecasting/tactical WFP, with a focus on medium- to long-term strategies. Strategic WFP aligns the workforce with business strategy over three to five years or more, focusing on skills development, talent mobility, and leadership needs. In contrast, recruitment forecasting centres on predicting immediate hiring needs rather than long-term skill development.

TABLE 4.1   Key differences between strategic and tactical WFP

Aspect	Strategic workforce planning (SWP)	Recruitment forecasting/ tactical workforce planning
Definition	A long-term, holistic approach to aligning workforce needs with business strategy	A short-to-medium-term process predicting hiring needs based on trends and data
Time Horizon	3–5 years or longer	12 months to 3 years
Focus	Workforce capability, skills development, and business transformation	Hiring volumes, timing, and talent availability
Scope	Broad – includes succession planning, talent mobility, and workforce trends	Narrow focus on filling roles based on demand
Data Sources	Business growth projections, market trends, demographic shifts	Historical hiring data, turnover rates, industry benchmarks
Technology Use	AI-driven analytics, scenario planning, workforce modelling	Applicant Tracking Systems (ATS), hiring trend analysis
Outcome	Future-proofing the organization with the right skills and talent	Ensuring short-term hiring needs are met efficiently

TABLE 4.1   *continued*

HR and Business Integration	Deeply linked to overall corporate strategy and transformation	More operational, supporting immediate talent acquisition needs
Example Activities	Identifying future skill gaps, workforce digitization, leadership succession planning	Predicting hiring needs for next year based on past turnover rates

Data sources for informing WFP decisions

When it comes to WFP, part of your role as an HR professional might be to gather available data and collaborate with business units to predict hiring needs. Say, for example, your organization is in the process of integrating WFP with business strategy. It needs to predict hiring needs over the next 12 months including for cyclical roles and seasonal staffing requirements, where there is likely repetition or turnover of roles. You could look at several data sources to determine future hiring needs:

- Business strategy – data about new markets, skills or geographies can help you understand the long-term vision for hiring needs. Use the business strategy to provide insights into strategic talent requirements identified in the business plan, aligned with the organization's long-term goals.
- HR/people strategy – data about cultural and competency changes can inform talent requirements as the organization evolves. Use the HR/people strategy to gather strategic and operational level talent requirements and insights.
- Historical TA or recruitment data – data about mission-critical roles, key dependent roles, hires or succession plans can provide insight into past hiring patterns. Use this data to gather trends on typical role types or hiring volumes based on previous years' performance data.

- Departmental/business unit plans – data about three-month tactical forecasts can provide detail about anticipated hiring needs. Use these plans to gather operational and tactical hiring needs from functional teams and key stakeholders.
- Process 'foresight' (requests, approvals, bids/wins) – data about headcount request and approval submissions can offer insight into the pre-approval process for headcount requests. Use this information to provide early signals for upcoming vacancies and to get a 'heads up' on imminent vacancies entering the pipeline.

You'll notice that this list of data sources progresses from strategic, long-term planning (such as business expansion and cultural shifts) to more tactical, short-term planning (such as immediate headcount requests and approvals). Combined, these data sources enable HR to build a comprehensive and forward-thinking workforce plan that aligns with both immediate needs and long-term business goals.

EXERCISE

Do some research in your own organization to understand which workforce strategy the business currently employs: operational WFP, recruitment forecasting or strategic WFP. Try to gain a clear picture of where your organization stands on its WFP journey:

- How does HR currently engage with senior leadership to align talent needs with business objectives?
- Is WFP more reactive and focused on operational needs?

If you don't have direct access to workforce strategy data, consider other data sources that can inform future hiring needs, such as those listed in the previous section. By gathering insights from these, you'll get a clearer picture of what's ahead, allowing you to anticipate and plan for the talent your organization will need.

   Use the checklist below to tick off which data sources you can access. Can you identify any gaps?

- Business strategy.
- HR/people strategy.
- Historical TA/recruitment data.
- Departmental plans/budgets.
- Process foresights.

Using data to develop a recruitment forecast

Once you've identified your available data sources, the next step is to start translating that insight into a recruitment forecast. As an HR professional, you play a key role in supporting TA by interpreting strategic data and surfacing the workforce signals that matter. Let's take a more detailed look at how each of the data sources just mentioned can inform your recruitment forecast and hiring plan.

BUSINESS STRATEGY

Identifying new markets, geographies and skills required.

- How will AI impact future skills and workforce requirements? Are new competencies/skills needed?
- Do we expect attrition/growth, and in which markets/disciplines?
- Are there projects on the horizon that need to be staffed?
- What are the current and anticipated talent gaps? What are the recruitment strategies that will fill these gaps?

HR/PEOPLE STRATEGY

Cultural or competency changes needed, attrition data, ageing workforce, etc.

- What is the current workforce composition? Is there an ageing population soon to retire that needs replenishing?

HISTORICAL TA/RECRUITMENT DATA

Consider typical role types, year-on-year hiring volumes, hires, and skills gaps. For example, if the organization is in a steady state without growth, is it safe to assume the previous years' demand as a baseline for the next year is a good starting point?

- What are the overall turnover rate and breakdown by department, role, and tenure?
- What is the projected attrition rate for the next year?
- Are there any areas of the business that have a noticeably higher turnover rate?

DEPARTMENT/BUSINESS FUNCTION PLANS

Look for succession plan gaps, departmental budgets, future hiring plans, and business growth.

EXERCISE

Once you've gathered insight from your organization's data sources, use the questions above as prompts to create a simple recruitment forecast.

WHAT WOULD YOU DO?
Number 5

Imagine you work in HR and have been asked to support TA to build a clearer picture of workforce needs over the next 3–5 years. There's growing concern that many employees are approaching retirement age, and this could lead to a shortage of critical skills across the organization. Your TA colleagues now need your help to understand what the future workforce might look like and how to prepare for it.

- What kind of data and insight could you provide to your TA colleagues to help them plan ahead?
- How could you prevent skills shortages to ensure there are no productivity gaps in the future?

CHAPTER SUMMARY

- WFP is the 'prefrontal cortex' of TA. Despite its importance, WFP is often overlooked, treated as an operational requirement and siloed outside of TA, making integration and impact difficult. TA is not just an operational function but a critical driver of long-term business success, aligning talent with future needs and strategic objectives.

- There are three different levels of WFP: strategic workforce planning (long-term, capability-focused), recruitment forecasting (mid-term, demand-driven), and operational planning (short-term, reactive).

- HR professionals need to move beyond reactive hiring by leveraging available data, business strategy, people plans, historical hiring, and budget insights to build a recruitment forecast and lay the foundation for longer-term planning.

REVIEW QUESTIONS

1 Describe six of the traditional principles behind strategic workforce planning.

2 What data can you gather to build a recruitment forecast?

3 Why is predicting the skills for the future through strategic workforce planning important for organizations?

Endnote

1 Satell, G (2014) A look back at why Blockbuster really failed and why it didn't have to, Forbes, 5 September, https://www.forbes.com/sites/gregsatell/2014/09/05/a-look-back-at-why-blockbuster-really-failed-and-why-it-didnt-have-to (archived at https://perma.cc/7A3S-3HAX)

CHAPTER FIVE

Employer branding

Introduction

The Introduction to this book talks about recruitment as both an art and a science, and you need both to get it right. This chapter describes part of the 'art' of the recruitment process. We look at a key TA building block that is vital to building the right quality of talent in the recruitment funnel – building and maintaining a strong employer brand.

An employer brand is the starting point for attracting, engaging and retaining talent. It influences almost every part of the TA lifecycle and is equally important to current employees as to prospective ones. While the science is in the structure of TA: workforce planning, data, assessment, and technology, the art is where the recruitment magic happens. This is where we tell stories to bring an employer's brand to life in a way that truly resonates with people.

We begin by looking at what an employer brand is and why it is important. We go on to explore the employee value proposition, what it means, why it is important and models you can use to create it. We end the chapter with an 'employer brand health check' that allows you to understand the strength of your own employer brand and where it could be improved.

LEARNING OBJECTIVES

By the end of this chapter, you will be able to:

- Explain the importance of a strong employer brand.

- Describe practical ways to strengthen your employer brand and employee value proposition.

- Understand the link between branding and candidate attraction and retention.

- Explain real-world strategies for improving talent attraction efforts.

Employer branding

Employer branding is the secret sauce that helps companies stand out from the crowd and attract the best talent, all while sparking creativity, forging emotional connections, and staying innovative. Employer branding describes the reputation and perception of a company as an employer in the market. It is a strategic process that focuses on shaping and promoting the company as a highly desirable place to work.

> **Employer branding:** A strategic process that aims to shape the reputation and perception of a company as an employer.

Employer branding aims to showcase the organization's culture, leadership, values and employee experience. A strong employer brand attracts candidates who align with the company's mission and values, positioning the organization as an 'employer of choice'. There are four primary goals of employer branding:

1 Attract top talent – showing the company as a great place to work helps bring in more qualified candidates who are excited to apply for jobs.

2 Improve employee retention – a strong employer brand makes employees feel valued and connected to the company, thereby reducing turnover.

3 Enhance employee engagement – when employees understand and connect with the company's values and work culture, they're more motivated and involved in their work and will be more productive. They are also more likely to advocate for their employer to their external talent.

4 Differentiate from competitors – a clear and positive employer brand helps the company stand out from other employers, making it easier to attract the best talent in the industry.

Employer branding is a critical building block in TA because it directly impacts how potential candidates perceive a company and whether they want to work there. Matthew Jeffrey, VP and global director of talent acquisition and attraction (formerly SAP, Bayer, and EY). says: 'AI is elevating organizations across the board, making it harder for any one company to stand out in the race for talent. As AI enhances all HR processes, the real differentiator – and greatest opportunity – will be employer branding.' Figure 5.1 shows a recruitment funnel and candidate journey, progressing from a candidate's awareness of an organization down through various stages to being made an offer and starting a job.

The employer brand sits at the very top of this model. It lays the groundwork for awareness and shapes the attraction and decision-making processes for candidates. As the figure demonstrates, a strong employer brand increases the likelihood that candidates will apply for roles. It serves as the first impression potential candidates have of the company. This initial perception attracts candidates even before the formal recruitment process begins.

Why is a strong employer brand important?

A negative employer brand can cost a company top talent and increase its recruitment costs. A survey by *Harvard Business*

FIGURE 5.1 The recruitment funnel and candidate journey

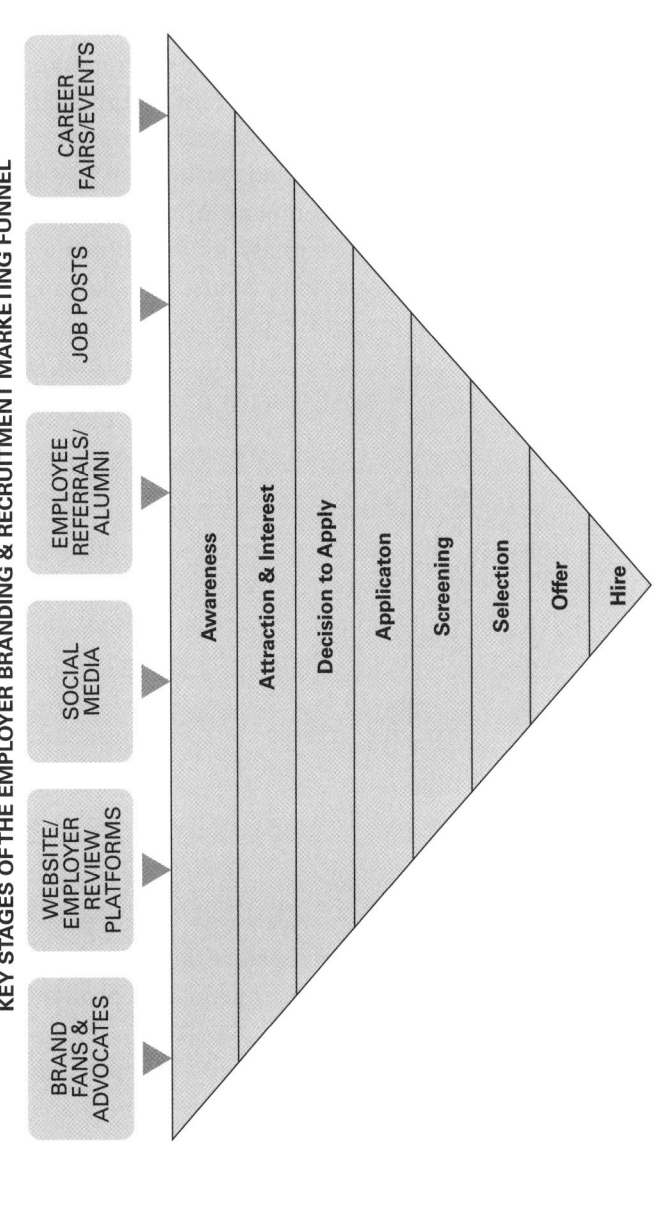

KEY STAGES OF THE EMPLOYER BRANDING & RECRUITMENT MARKETING FUNNEL

BRAND FANS & ADVOCATES

WEBSITE/ EMPLOYER REVIEW PLATFORMS

SOCIAL MEDIA

EMPLOYEE REFERRALS/ ALUMNI

JOB POSTS

CAREER FAIRS/EVENTS

Awareness

Attraction & Interest

Decision to Apply

Applicaton

Screening

Selection

Offer

Hire

Review found that a poor reputation can increase hiring costs. Even if a company offers a higher salary, candidates may be hesitant to work there if the employer brand is negative. The survey showed that if a company with a bad reputation raised salaries by 10 per cent, only 28 per cent of candidates would still consider applying for the job.[1]

You don't have to look far to find examples of how a negative employer brand can harm a company. Amazon has faced heavy public criticism over how it treats its warehouse operatives, with issues like high stress, long hours, and demanding productivity targets. After negative press attention, Amazon had difficulty attracting workers for warehouse roles and saw higher turnover rates. This, in turn, affected productivity and overall company performance.[2]

USING YOUR EMPLOYER BRAND TO TELL STORIES

Stories draw people in. They attract attention and evoke emotion. This is what great employer branding strategies are all about: telling authentic stories that create a visual identity that truly resonates with people. Unfortunately, many organizations get it wrong. They can fail to establish that crucial emotional connection, or worse, their message just isn't authentic. To illustrate this, let's consider some examples where brands alienated female consumers through inauthentic and insensitive storytelling.

In 2021, Burger King sent an ironic, provocative tweet on International Women's Day, which was intended to highlight that only 20 per cent of chefs were women. It read, 'Women Belong in the Kitchen'. The tweet, intended to promote women in the culinary industry and a new scholarship programme for female chefs – a great strategy in itself – immediately faced a huge backlash. What was meant to be ironic and a great way of supporting its female staff, ended up coming across as tone-deaf and insensitive. The scholarship programme was an employer brand initiative, but Burger King's execution damaged both internal morale and external reputation as an inclusive employer.

Another example is Dove's 2017 controversy. In an attempt to celebrate inclusivity, it released an advert featuring a black woman removing her shirt to reveal a white woman underneath. This was widely criticized as racially insensitive, implying that lighter skin tones were more desirable. While Dove had a history of championing diversity, this campaign missed the mark and sparked a major backlash among Dove's potential customers: women.[3]

Both these brands made serious missteps. The controversial advert from Dove sent a confusing message to both consumers and potential employees about its inclusive values. *Forbes* reports that women drive 70 to 80 per cent of all consumer purchasing decisions.[4] This substantial influence underscores the importance for brands to engage thoughtfully with female consumers to avoid potential negative reactions, which could harm the brand's reputation.

Employer brands must be treated with delicacy to ensure they connect emotionally and authentically with audiences. When done right, a great employer brand can create a lasting impression. When done badly, it can have severe repercussions and hiring consequences for the business. This disconnect often comes down to a lack of a clear and compelling employee value proposition, which we will go on to consider now.

The employee value proposition (EVP)

Employee value proposition (EVP): The unique set of benefits, rewards and experiences an employer offers to employees in exchange for their skills, capabilities and commitment.

Simply having an employer brand isn't enough. Companies also need a clear employee value proposition (EVP) to attract the top talent. In the simplest terms, an EVP is what an employer offers to an employee. It encompasses the tangible benefits (perks and salary) and involves emotional factors such as the company culture and values that motivate employees to work for you. The EVP is the core element of your employer brand strategy. It guides how your organization presents itself to potential applicants, helps shape your company culture and defines who you are as an employer through your values, behaviours, and principles.

Without a clear EVP, companies risk sending inconsistent messages that may attract candidates who don't align with the company's values or culture. On the other hand, a well-articulated EVP ensures that your key messaging resonates with the right talent, strengthening your ability to attract candidates who share your company's vision and values.

The Give and Get Model

A strong EVP communicates the unique benefits, values, and experiences employees can expect, while also setting clear expectations of what the company seeks in return, ensuring mutual fit between the organization and its talent. For example, some organizations, such as Google, Netflix, Salesforce and Microsoft, have defined their EVP using the Give and Get Model, a framework that clearly defines the mutual exchange between the employer and employee. It highlights what the company offers to its employees (the 'give') and what the company expects in return (the 'get').

Examples of what companies 'give' to employees:

- Compensation – competitive salary, bonuses, benefits.
- Career development – opportunities for growth, training and advancement.
- Work environment – supportive culture, inclusive teams, healthy work–life balance.
- Job security – stability and clear professional paths.
- Purpose and values – alignment with the organization's mission, values and sense of purpose.

Examples of what companies 'get' from employees:

- Performance and contribution – high-quality work, meeting productivity and goals.
- Engagement – active participation, enthusiasm and commitment to the company's objectives.
- Culture fit – alignment with a company's values and culture.
- Innovation and ideas – creativity and problem-solving.
- Collaboration – teamwork, communication and collaboration with colleagues.

STOP AND THINK

Think about the 'give and get' dynamic at your own organization. Is it balanced, with employer and employee receiving and giving equally? Consider aspects such as company culture, job security and salary. Do you have different demographics with varying expectations and requirements? Particularly around values, communication and cultural sensitivity?

The Four Pillars Model

The Give and Get Model isn't the only framework used by organization to define the structure of the EVP. Another is the Four Pillars Model, which is a popular and more streamlined approach as it breaks the EVP into four key areas or 'pillars', as shown in Figure 5.2:

1 Culture and values.
2 Career development.
3 Work–life balance.
4 Compensation and benefits.

Organizations often work with employer branding agencies to choose the right EVP model that addresses the unique challenges they face. Some companies may prioritize work–life balance and

FIGURE 5.2   The Four Pillars Model for defining the EVP

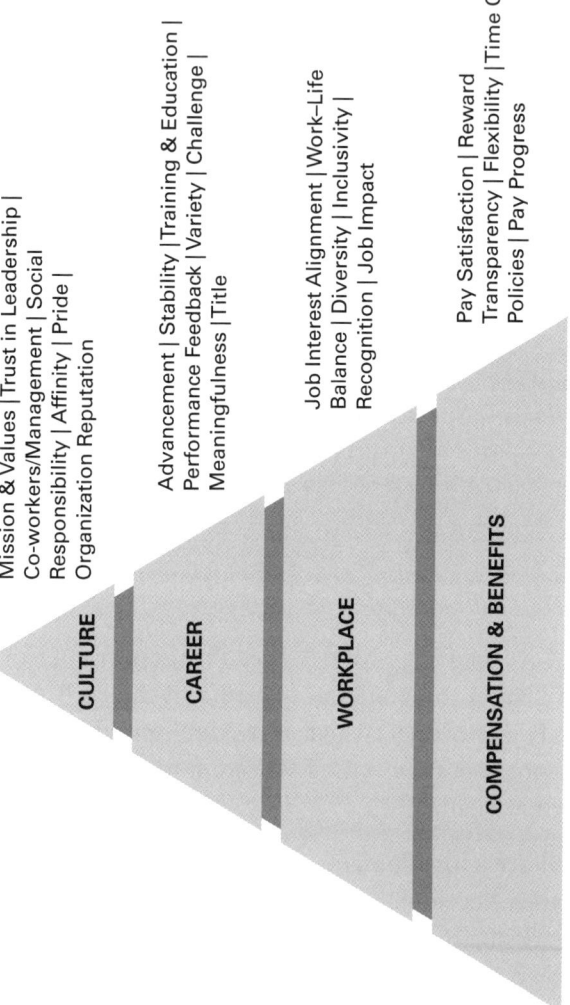

CULTURE

Mission & Values | Trust in Leadership | Co-workers/Management | Social Responsibility | Affinity | Pride | Organization Reputation

CAREER

Advancement | Stability | Training & Education | Performance Feedback | Variety | Challenge | Meaningfulness | Title

WORKPLACE

Job Interest Alignment | Work–Life Balance | Diversity | Inclusivity | Recognition | Job Impact

COMPENSATION & BENEFITS

Pay Satisfaction | Reward Transparency | Flexibility | Time Off | Policies | Pay Progress employee well-being, while others might focus more on career advancement and competitive compensation. In most cases, organizations will blend elements from different conceptual and theoretical models to create a comprehensive and appealing EVP that resonates with their intended candidate audience, or the specific problem it's trying to solve.

Whichever model an organization decides on, its EVP must be authentic, resonate with the target audience and reflect the true culture, values and purpose of the organization. Misrepresenting the company or creating a false perception can lead to disengagement and high turnover. New employees may feel misled, which will ultimately impact future recruitment and retention efforts. The examples in the box show how misrepresenting a company through its EVP can go wrong. The first is of the retailer, Gap, and the second is of a leading professional services firm. Both demonstrate why an employer's EVP should be carefully considered before launching any recruitment marketing campaigns or job advertisements.

EXAMPLES

Gap fails to reflect its true culture and values:

- **Problem:** Gap's EVP message used to emphasize work–life balance with a strong message suggesting that it provided flexible hours and a supportive culture and work environment – 'We're all about balance'. However, employees frequently reported longer hours, high expectations and little flexibility in practice, which contradicted the EVP messaging.

- **Impact:** This perceived inconsistency led to frustration and disengagement, particularly among younger workers who valued work–life balance and flexibility. The mismatch between the message and the actual employee experience eroded trust in the brand and contributed to high turnover rates.

A leading consulting firm gets cultural resonance wrong:

- **Problem:** A global employer value proposition (EVP) with a theme centred on 'improving the world of work' performed well globally but failed to resonate with certain local audiences – particularly younger job seekers in a different regional market. The company failed to consider local language nunances, which might impact specific audiences. At regional UK career fairs, for example, students often misinterpreted the word 'building' in the message as a reference to the construction industry, when in fact, the organization operates in professional services.

- **Issue:** This kind of misalignment can directly impact potential candidates' understanding of the company's core business, leading to a lack of interest or confusion, particularly from individuals who might not see a fit for their skills. As a result, it could deter some candidates, especially younger or diverse talent from applying altogether.

When developing an EVP, remember it's also crucial for an organization's internal and external messaging to align, so that the way your current employees perceive the organization matches how external candidates view you. When both are in sync, you create a more consistent and authentic employer brand, and avoid mistakes like the one Gap made (refer to the example box).

How to develop an EVP

As an early career professional in HR or TA, you may be asked to work on an EVP development project, so it's a great idea to understand how this messaging framework comes together.

Figure 5.3 is an EVP framework giving a structured approach to defining and communicating what makes your organization an exceptional place to work.

'Core positioning' is at the centre. This is the one key quality you want to be known for that resonates with current employees and prospective candidates, and informs the entire employer brand. Within this core are typically three to five key pillars, such as work–life balance, purpose, and opportunity, all of which are crucial in shaping the overall employee experience.

FIGURE 5.3 A framework for developing an EVP

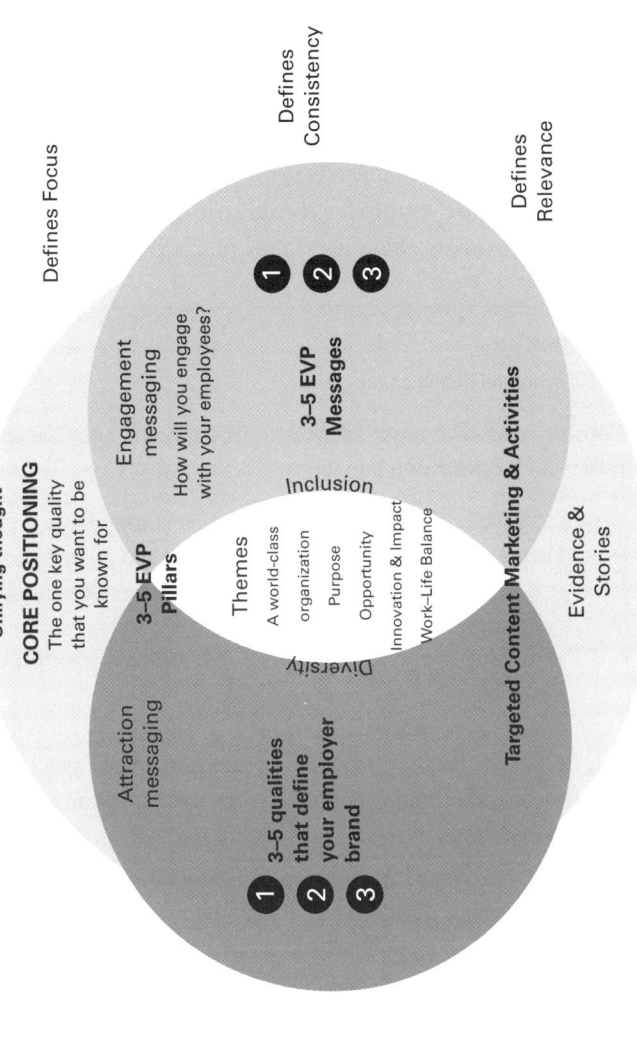

Each pillar has key attraction and engagement messaging aligned to it (we discuss attraction in Chapter 6). The attraction messaging gives three to five key qualities that define your employer brand, while the engagement messaging gives three to five EVP messages, showing how you will engage with employees. The attract and engage segments show how the organization can effectively target the right talent while ensuring they connect with the company's values.

Additionally, the framework emphasizes the importance of highlighting your employer brand through targeted content marketing, ensuring these messages reach the right audience.

EXERCISE
Employer brand health check

Consider your own organization's employer brand and EVP and reflect on the following questions.

1 Are you facing any attraction or retention challenges?
    – How well is your organization attracting top talent?
    – Are you having trouble filling open positions with quality candidates?
    – Is employee turnover high or do you struggle to retain key employees?
    – Could these challenges be linked to your employer brand or EVP? For example, do new hires or existing employees feel there's a mismatch between what was promised and their actual experience?

2 How is your organization perceived externally?
    – What might people outside the organization say about your company as an employer?
    – Consider the candidate perspective: what impression would someone form based on your website, Glassdoor reviews or word-of-mouth?
    – If you've recently joined the organization, reflect on your initial perception.

- Can you clearly describe your company's purpose and value proposition?
- Does your employer brand generate positive word-of-mouth?

3 How clearly defined is your EVP?
- Does your organization have a distinct, well-articulated EVP?
- Can you express it easily and confidently?
- Is the EVP reflected across recruitment materials, onboarding, internal communications, and the day-to-day employee experience?
- Are the promises made consistent with what employees experience?

4 How consistent is your external messaging?
- Review your careers website, social media channels, and job adverts.
- Are your employer brand and EVP clearly communicated consistently across all candidate touchpoints?
- Do your messages resonate with the type of candidates you're aiming to attract?
- Are your company culture and values showcased authentically and engagingly?

5 Is your employer brand aligned with your core values?
- Do your values align with your EVP and broader employer brand?
- Are these values consistently promoted both internally and externally?
- Do employees genuinely live these values in their day-to-day work?

6 What's missing from your current employer brand strategy?
- Is there a gap in how your organization presents itself as an employer?
- Are there key moments, such as the candidate journey or onboarding process, that could be improved?
- What's one area that, if improved, could significantly boost your reputation as an employer?

7 Where do you see opportunities for improvement in your employer brand?
   – What small change could make the most immediate impact on your employer brand?
   – Could this be through clearer EVP communication, improved internal advocacy, or a more engaging candidate experience?

8 Actionable next steps:
   – Based on your reflections, what strategies or initiatives could you implement to enhance your employer brand?
   – How can you collaborate with TA (if you work in HR), Comms, or business leaders to move these ideas?

CHAPTER SUMMARY

- Employer branding is a critical TA building block, because it directly impacts how the company is perceived and whether people want to work there.

- A negative employer brand can have serious consequences for a company. People often care more about the employer brand than benefits such as salary.

- It's important to bring your employer brand to life through authentic and sensitive storytelling.

- An EVP is the core element of your employer brand strategy, showing what employees get for working at the company. It encompasses tangible elements such as salary and benefits and intangible ones such as company culture.

- An EVP needs to be carefully crafted and demonstrate the key qualities you want to be known for by both prospective and current employees.

REVIEW QUESTIONS

1 Why is employer branding vital if you want to attract and retain good talent?

2 Outline two consequences of having a negative employer brand.

3 Name two key messages your EVP needs to give to prospective and current employees.

Endnotes

1 Burgess, W (2016) A bad reputation costs a company at least 10% more per hire, *Harvard Business Review*, 29 March, https://hbr.org/2016/03/a-bad-reputation-costs-company-at-least-10-more-per-hire (archived at https://perma.cc/DM74-36L7)

2 TUC (nd) Challenging Amazon report – Criticisms of Amazon, https://www.tuc.org.uk/node/523929 (archived at https://perma.cc/M4XV-M6R5)

3 Astor, M (2017) Dove drops an ad accused of racism, *The New York Times*, 8 October, https://www.nytimes.com/2017/10/08/business/dove-ad-racist.html (archived at https://perma.cc/WUL2-W8KA)

4 Davis, K M (2019) 20 facts and figures to know when marketing to women, *Forbes*, 13 May, https://www.forbes.com/sites/forbescontentmarketing/2019/05/13/20-facts-and-figures-to-know-when-marketing-to-women/ (archived at https://perma.cc/BR44-XU69)

CHAPTER SIX

Candidate attraction and sourcing

Introduction

This chapter introduces candidate attraction and sourcing, the next TA building block. This building block aligns with two stages of the TA lifecycle – 'Attract' and 'Engage/source'. Getting your employer brand and EVP right (the subject of the last chapter) is crucial to attract and source candidates. The employer brand, EVP and sourcing strategies work together to actively engage candidates. Through engagement, awareness turns into interest and interest turns into connection.

This chapter begins by looking at what candidate attraction is and three channels organizations typically use to do it. We progress to look at how organizations are starting to use more innovative channels to attract talent, such as talent communities and employee advocacy programmes. We progress to consider sourcing strategies and how to craft a 'source mix' that draws from the broadest possible pool and focuses on attracting diverse talent. We consider the difference between active candidates – those who are looking for work – and passive ones – those who aren't actively looking, but who might be tempted into the perfect role. We also look at how to address talent loss, and the importance of nurturing those 'near misses' who do not make it through the selection process (the topic of Chapter 7). Finally, we consider the importance of Boolean search as a foundational skill for all HR and TA practitioners.

LEARNING OBJECTIVES

By the end of this chapter, you will be able to:

- List some of the innovative ways TA teams attract top talent.
- Explain how EVP, attraction and sourcing result in engagement.
- Describe how to craft a strategic source mix that draws from the widest possible talent pool.
- Understand the difference between active and passive candidates and how to recycle and nurture both.
- Perform Boolean searches to elevate your sourcing capabilities.

Candidate attraction

Candidate attraction: The tactical strategies designed to capture candidates' attention for open job roles.

In the 'Attract' stage of the TA lifecycle, potential candidates are actively engaged and encouraged to apply through a compelling EVP. This stage comes into play once a strong employer brand has been established and focuses on directly engaging the target audience through tailored recruitment messaging, job postings, employer content, career fairs and more.

The goal of this phase is to raise awareness of open roles, spark candidates' curiosity and inspire them to engage with your recruitment campaigns, ultimately leading them to apply. This is where TA teams play a crucial role, mobilizing roles and aligning relevant recruitment marketing and sourcing strategies. Traditionally, TA teams rely on three channel strategies:

1 Internal channels – leveraging internal mobility and career advancement, and tapping into employees as ambassadors for recommending potential candidates.
2 Direct external channels – directly engaging prospective employees by leveraging the company's employer brand, website, job boards and social media platforms.
3 Indirect channels – using third-party suppliers, such as recruitment agencies, search firms and outreach programmes, to help find and attract potential candidates.

However, the landscape of recruitment channels is evolving, and many organizations are using innovative ways to attract top talent.

Innovative ways to attract top talent

As technology evolves, innovative approaches to candidate attraction are replacing traditional methods. These move beyond attraction to engagement, focusing on building meaningful relationships with candidates.

- Direct channels:
  - Talent communities: Beyond just passive job seekers, talent pools or communities of individuals who've expressed interest in your company but haven't yet applied can be nurtured and engaged continuously.
  - Social media advertising and influencer marketing: Platforms like LinkedIn, Instagram, and TikTok offer highly targeted opportunities to reach specific demographics and audiences with internal and external influencers.
- Indirect channel:
  - Employee advocacy programmes: Going beyond referrals, smarter organizations are now involving their employees to share job postings and company culture content on their personal networks, amplifying the company's reach.

As we saw in Chapter 5, a strong employer brand is an invaluable tool for attracting top talent and influencing candidates' decisions to apply. However, strategies must be tailored to reach a broader and more diverse pool of candidates. While activation campaigns can certainly help increase brand awareness and draw talent in certain fields or locations, they may not always address specific talent skill needs or fill geographic gaps. In some cases, certain roles or locations may have a lower concentration of qualified candidates, resulting in fewer applications or mismatched role fits.

To overcome these challenges, it's crucial to continuously review, refine, and expand your recruitment strategy. A targeted approach that balances cost-efficiency, candidate quality, and time is essential for attracting the right talent to the right roles. Striking the right balance between time, cost and quality is challenging. For instance, if a hiring manager has an urgent need for a difficult-to-fill role needing highly specialized technical skills in a challenging location, the most effective route to market may be through a specialist agency, or indirect channel.

Meanwhile, the TA team can focus on building a longer-term talent strategy, such as creating a graduate programme or developing a proactive talent pipeline or community. Sourcing channels are fundamental in supporting and amplifying your employer brand. The strategic use of these channels can greatly influence how your company is perceived by potential candidates and how effectively you attract and engage top talent. Figure 6.1 shows how different sourcing channels can support and enhance your employer brand.

How EVP, attraction, and sourcing result in engagement

In Chapter 5, we explored the foundational elements of employer brand and EVP – two critical components of a connected framework. Let's now examine how they operate as part of a broader talent engagement ecosystem that results in talent engagement.

FIGURE 6.1   Using sourcing channels to support your employer brand

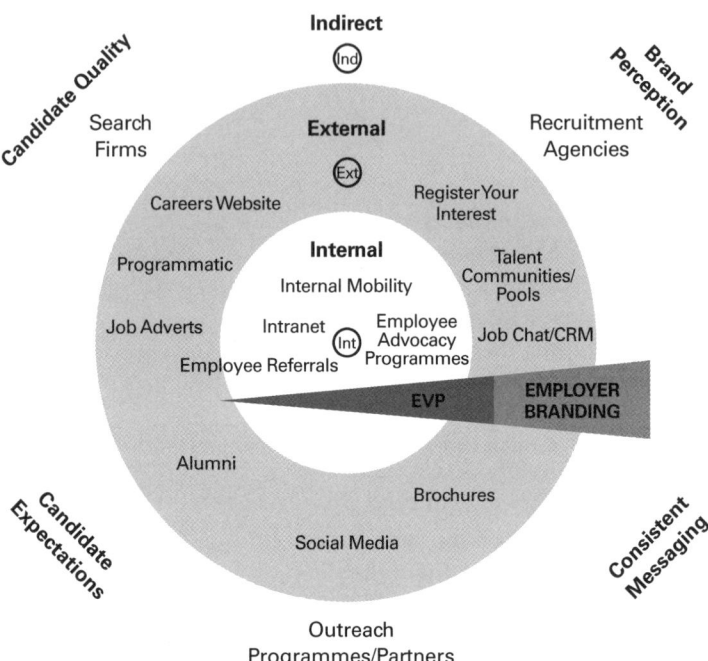

Talent engagement: The heart of any effective employer branding strategy is successful talent engagement. This is how the organization effectively attracts, connects with, and retains potential and existing employees by communicating and delivering upon its EVP and promise.

Imagine you are designing a talent ecosystem for your organization. You need a framework that demonstrates how your talent engagement strategy evolves, from defining your brand identity to creating human connections. This starts with a clear sense of who you are, ultimately culminating in authentic interactions with talent.

At the top, the employer brand shapes how your organization is perceived in the external talent market. It tells the story of who you are, what you stand for, and why you matter, setting the tone for how you show up as an employer of choice.

At the centre sits your EVP, a clear and authentic articulation of what you offer in return for the skills, energy, and commitment of your people. It answers the key question: Why should someone choose to join and stay with you?

From there, your employer brand and EVP come to life through targeted attraction and sourcing strategies. These ensure your message reaches the right audiences, in the right places, with the right tone – through curated content, tailored campaigns, and sourcing methods that reflect your values and culture.

The outcome of this interconnected approach is engagement, where awareness turns into interest, and interest turns into connection. It's about building trust, emotional resonance, and meaningful relationships with talent from the very first interaction. Figure 6.2 shows this talent ecosystem.

Candidate sourcing strategies

Sourcing strategy: A comprehensive plan that outlines the methods and channels used to identify, attract and engage potential candidates for roles within an organization.

The goal of a sourcing strategy is to build a diverse, high-quality talent pool, engage with potential candidates effectively and reduce the time and cost to hire, all while aligning with the company's overall hiring needs and business objectives. Best practice candidate sourcing strategies involve a proactive, systematic approach to identifying, attracting and engaging with potential candidates. They determine where to find candidates, how to engage with them and how to create a talent pipeline.

FIGURE 6.2   How employer brand, EVP and sourcing culminate in engagement

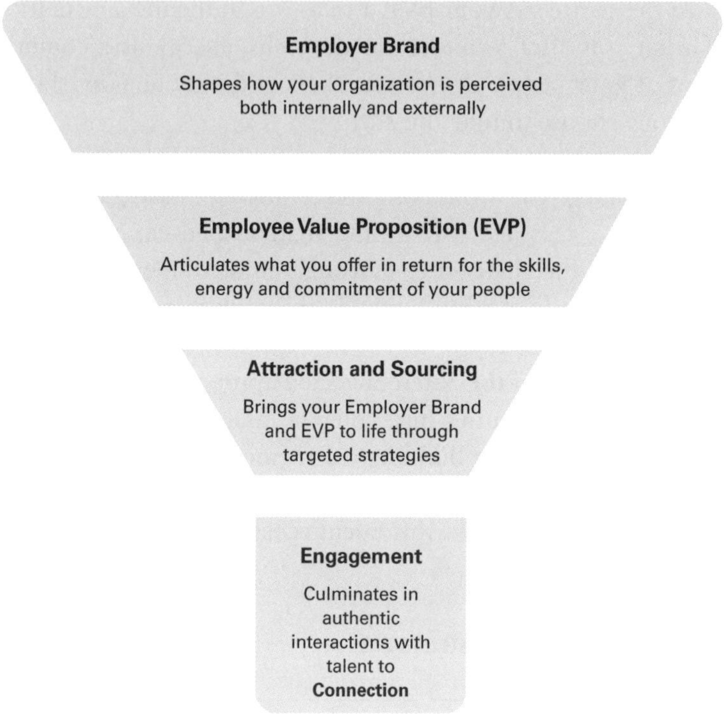

Employer Brand

Shapes how your organization is perceived both internally and externally

Employee Value Proposition (EVP)

Articulates what you offer in return for the skills, energy and commitment of your people

Attraction and Sourcing

Brings your Employer Brand and EVP to life through targeted strategies

Engagement

Culminates in authentic interactions with talent to **Connection**

Whether you work in HR or TA, you play an essential role in continuously supporting strategic sourcing. This helps reduce reliance on agency spend, increases quality of hiring, and minimizes the need for reactive recruitment.

A great sourcing strategy is proactive and systematic, ensuring that talent gaps are identified and addressed before they become urgent. It is typically aligned with strategic workforce plans and clearly defined organizational needs. By anticipating future hiring requirements, a sourcing strategy helps the organization stay ahead of talent shortages, ensuring that the right candidates are always available when needed. Whether through talent intelligence, market analysis, or strategic WFP, a strong sourcing strategy enables a company to be agile, competitive and prepared for both current and future hiring demands.

Imagine the following scenario. A business plans to open a new site or launch a new product globally, but is unsure of the best location for future talent. In this scenario, strategic WFP can be leveraged alongside talent intelligence techniques to identify key global locations with a strong talent pool. These techniques involve analysing market trends, labour availability and skill sets in different regions to ensure the company can access the critical skills required and gain competitive talent advantage. By using data-driven insights, the business can strategically choose the optimal location to ensure it has a sustainable talent pipeline, ensuring that the future workforce aligns with both business needs and market conditions.

Less sophisticated and more straightforward activities involve ensuring the right mix of sourcing channels. These channels might include job boards, social media, employee referrals, internal mobility and recruitment agencies, all chosen based on the role's specific requirements, urgency and/or the type of candidates being sought (active or passive – we cover this later in the chapter). The ultimate goal is to ensure that the organization is always prepared with a strong, diverse talent pool, ready to meet current and future hiring needs.

The art of crafting a strategic source mix

You've already grasped the various sourcing channels, but here's where it gets truly exciting.

The creativity in TA comes from how you blend and leverage these channels together to meet your company's strategic goals. It's not just about filling open roles; it's about proactively creating a balanced 'source mix' that aligns with the future needs of the business. When this is done correctly, this makes the TA role not only more strategic but also much more dynamic.

> **Source mix:** A sourcing strategy that taps into a variety of channels to attract the best talent from the broadest possible pool.

In organizations with a forward-thinking recruitment strategy, sourcing is a purposeful, well-structured effort. These companies don't solely rely on obvious channels such as career websites (even though those are essential!). Instead, they focus on creating a thoughtful mix of sourcing methods that align with the company's long-term goals. This strategy does not rely on posting job ads and waiting for candidates to apply; it's more about adopting a thoughtful go-to-market strategy that taps into a variety of channels to attract the best candidates from the broadest possible talent pool.

A well-crafted source mix ensures that candidates come from diverse channels, encouraging diverse backgrounds, whether through employee referrals, internal mobility, or recruitment agencies. Each channel should be optimized based on the specific role requirements.

Relying too heavily on one sourcing channel introduces significant recruitment and talent risks, which is why organizations should strive for a balanced source mix. It could lead to 'groupthink', where candidates of a similar type dominate the pool by non-diverse employees, limiting diversity and innovation. It can also result in an overuse of agencies, driving up recruitment costs unnecessarily.

> **TOP TIP**
> Include internal candidates in the source mix
>
> Ensure that internal candidates are given access to opportunities first. Current employees can feel demotivated if they see roles being filled externally rather than through internal growth opportunities. This can negatively impact morale and lead to higher turnover, ultimately causing the loss of valuable talent.

STOP AND THINK

Do some research in your organization to understand which channels you source candidates through, and your source mix. Consider the following questions:

1 What channels are you using?
   - Are there any you're not using that could be beneficial (e.g. social media influencers, talent communities)?
2 Which channels are working well?
   - Are you effectively leveraging the best-performing channels for quality candidates?
   - Is diversity or reaching certain demographics still a key challenge, and how will your organization reach a broader church of talent?
3 Are you over-reliant on any channels?
   - Are you overly dependent on agencies or other external sources? How can you reduce this reliance?
   - How does the use of agency channels compare to direct hiring channels in terms of cost-effectiveness?
4 How can you better support TA efforts?
   - What internal tools, resources, or strategies (e.g. talent pools, recruitment marketing) can strengthen your process?
5 Is your organization ready for new channels?
   - Have you explored innovative approaches like employee advocacy or social media influencers to broaden your reach?
   - Do you have a referral programme, and can it be better communicated or elevated to maximize its impact?

Sourcing checklist:

1 Review the channels you're currently using.
2 Identify any gaps or underutilized channels.
3 Assess channel performance and effectiveness.
4 Check your reliance on external sources (e.g. agencies).
5 Consider new, innovative channels for future recruitment.

Active and passive candidates

In addition to thinking about different types of channels, it's essential to consider how we target the various types of candidates available through them.

A key distinction lies in whether candidates are actively seeking work (active talent) or not currently looking (passive talent).

> **Active talent:** Candidates who are actively seeking work

> **Passive talent:** Candidates who are not actively seeking work but who may be open to the right role should it come along.

Active candidates are engaged in the job market and actively applying to open roles. They tend to respond quickly to job opportunities and show clear interest. However, they might not always be the best cultural or long-term fit for your organization. Passive candidates are not actively seeking a new role, but they may be open to opportunities if the right role comes along. While passive candidates can offer a high potential fit, they typically come with a longer recruitment cycle. It's much harder to hook their interest and engagement.

There is no one-size-fits-all solution; the best approach depends on the role and hiring needs. For urgent, high-volume roles, active candidates may be the better choice due to their immediate availability. For highly specialized or hard-to-fill positions, passive candidates often make the best fit, as they bring valuable expertise but require a more strategic, long-term approach.

In an employer-driven market (see Chapter 1), there may be a larger pool of active candidates, while in a candidate-driven market, passive candidates can be more discerning, harder to engage, and may require more effort to attract. They may also be tied into longer-term retention strategies with their firms.

Addressing talent loss

Recruitment processes can sometimes leak great candidates, particularly diverse talents. Think of your recruitment process like filling a bucket with talent every time you advertise or source for a role. If that bucket has a hole, because you're not capturing, storing, or re-engaging candidates effectively, then valuable talent is going to slip right through it. And nobody wants a leaky bucket.

Valuable talent can be lost at various stages of the TA life-cycle. In Chapter 7, we consider candidate assessment and selection, and talent loss in terms of those candidates who apply and don't get selected. These may be candidates who were silver medallists in the interview process, potential speculative superstars, or passive talent gems uncovered during sourcing. Sophisticated TA teams with a strong focus on the candidate experience understand the importance of staying connected with candidates who apply but aren't successful for a role. It's vital to keep these candidates in the loop and nurture them for future opportunities.

Recycling and nurturing candidates is a key part of building a sustainable future talent pipeline. This involves maintaining relationships with top talent, even when there isn't an immediate vacancy, so that you can re-engage them when the right role arises.

We'll dig deeper into this idea when we talk assessment strategy in Chapter 7, and how to avoid talent loss, or a leaky bucket, in the assessment and selection process, but for now, ask yourself: Is your organization capturing every opportunity to build your future talent pipeline, or are you letting great candidates drain away?

Sourcing methods for sustainable recruitment

1. Vacancy advertising on employer career site

What is it?

- A reactive strategy targeting 'active' job seekers.

Typical impact and timeline:

- Short term: one to four weeks.

How is it done?

- Advertising via your employer career site.
- Writing compelling search-friendly job adverts, and publishing to your careers page and job boards.

2. Proactive candidate sourcing

What is it?

- A precision-based approach that targets passive talent.
- This requires stronger TA capabilities, and sometimes, dedicated sourcing teams to target hard-to-reach talent. Rather than waiting for candidates to apply, sourcing experts directly seek out and engage individuals directly.

Typical impact and timeline:

- Varies depending on role complexity and market availability.

How is it done?

- Uses Boolean searches, LinkedIn, niche platforms such as GitHub/Stack Overflow, referrals and professional networks. Tailored outreach by sourcing specialists to engage talent with messaging to attract interest. These candidates are not generally visible through traditional sourcing methods.
- By reaching out to this untapped pool of candidates, organizations can connect with highly qualified professionals

who may be the perfect fit for critical roles, even if they're not currently job hunting (passive talent).

3. Talent pooling

What is it?

- Building pipelines for future-fit talent, whether they have applied for a role or not.
- Helps reduce time-to-hire and prepare for future recruitment needs.
- These candidates tend to be warm, have expressed an interest in the employer brand, and thereby proactively maintaining them into a pool will cultivate a strong pipeline of already engaged talent.

Typical impact and timeline:

- Medium to long term.

How is it done?

- Pool silver medallists, warm candidates, and speculative interest into your CRM or ATS.
- Often recruiters do this behind the scenes, proactively engaging with candidates and putting them into a searchable database. Candidate pools include speculative applicants, passive candidates, and previous applicants who fit future needs.

4. Candidate nurturing

What is it?

- A long-term engagement strategy aimed at building relationships with potential candidates over time.
- Often used in early careers or hard-to-fill talent segments.

Typical impact and timeline:

- Long term.

How is it done?

- Run email campaigns, host events, share branded content, and maintain regular engagement.

STOP AND THINK

Which of the four strategies listed in this section are you using effectively in your business today? Consider the following questions and how you could use any of these strategies to address any issues:

1   Are there roles in your business that feel impossible to fill?

2   Are you constantly hiring for the same roles again and again?

3   Are there positions with high dependency on technical skills?

4   Are your TA teams burning out while waiting for the 'right' person to apply, leaving seats empty, and the business frustrated, because the talent just isn't there?

Based on your reflections, what actions and conversations should happen next?

Whether you work in HR or TA, your influence is pivotal. You can help your TA colleagues drive the business case for a more strategic approach, one that acknowledges that attracting and retaining the right talent requires more than just posting a job ad and hoping for the best. Things you can do:

- Champion TA as a driver of organizational performance.

- Support your TA peers and colleagues in building trust through a more proactive and data-driven strategic approach.

- Shift mindsets from reactive hiring to workforce planning, talent pipelining and long-term value creation.

> **TOP TIP**
> Use a net and a rod
>
> Hiring is a bit like going fishing with a net versus a fancy rod.
>   Imagine you're heading out on a fishing trip, determined to catch that perfect freshwater trout for supper. You could cast a net, which is like posting your job advert. And hey, you might just get lucky and scoop up the perfect trout of your dreams. It's quite unlikely, as it needs to be swimming by at the right moment.
>   The smarter trout is further afield, deeper in the stream, not cruising past your net at the exact time that you have cast it. That's when you need to invest in a fishing rod – a targeted, proactive approach to seek out and reel in exactly what you're looking for. Smart hiring means doing both, using a net and a rod. The net to capture active fish (candidates), and the rod (proactive sourcing) to land the hard-to-reach, valuable fish (candidates) further afield.

The TA maturity model and talent sourcing

The best TA teams aren't just filling roles; they're nurturing talent ecosystems. You can understand your organization's current level of sourcing maturity using the TA maturity model introduced in Chapter 3 by using the following five levels:

1 Initial/reactive – basic sourcing: Relying mainly on career websites and job boards, with minimal proactive sourcing.
2 Defined – external focus: Heavy reliance on third-party recruiters and paid advertising, with limited internal sourcing.
3 Integrated – internal mobility: Shifting focus to create internal opportunities, supplemented by external hires.
4 Strategic – advanced talent communities: Building and nurturing talent pools through data-driven processes and industry partnerships.

5 AI-driven sourcing: Using AI tools to proactively rank and identify best-fit candidates, automate talent pooling and forecast hiring needs.

> **STOP AND THINK**
>
> Which level of the TA maturity model does your organization sit at, when it comes to talent sourcing?

Boolean basics: A must-have skill

Boolean search is a foundational skill for all HR and TA practitioners, especially if you are early in your career. Knowing how to do it well can significantly elevate your sourcing capabilities. Boolean logic helps you go beyond the surface of databases, job boards, and platforms like LinkedIn to uncover hidden or passive talent that might not appear through standard keyword searches or traditional job ads.

Boolean search uses a structured combination of keywords and operators, primarily; AND, OR, and NOT, to refine and target search results. For example:

- Use AND to narrow your search by combining criteria (e.g. 'Java AND Python' returns profiles with both).
- Use OR to expand your reach across similar skill sets or job titles (e.g. 'Accountant OR CIMA').
- Use NOT to exclude irrelevant results (e.g. 'Marketing NOT Sales').

These searches can be performed across your ATS (Applicant Tracking System), CRM, LinkedIn Recruiter, or niche databases, making Boolean one of the most versatile and low-cost sourcing tools in your toolkit.

In practice, Boolean logic is typically seen as a recruiter's responsibility. However, for HR professionals whose roles intersect with TA, developing this skill can be incredibly valuable.

- Reduce time-to-hire by quickly zeroing in on suitable candidates.
- Discover underrepresented or non-traditional talent by searching outside standard job boards.
- Build more strategic pipelines, especially when working in competitive or skills-scarce markets.
- Encourage the business to collaborate with the recruitment team by providing clear, targeted keywords that define the essential criteria for narrowing down candidate searches.

By embedding Boolean search skills early in your career, you set yourself apart as a proactive talent partner, not just relying on applications but shaping who enters the recruitment process.

EXERCISE

Test your Boolean search skills. Look for a graduate engineer in London or the Greater London area, but not an intern. Write a Boolean search string for LinkedIn and test it using the LinkedIn search bar. How many talents can you find?

WHAT WOULD YOU DO?
Number 6

You have been asked to source a Data Analyst with SQL and Tableau skills. Where would you look to source one, and what Boolean search phrases would you use?

CHAPTER SUMMARY

- Sourcing is a proactive process of finding and engaging potential candidates before roles become urgent, not just advertising jobs.
- Effective sourcing includes a mix of traditional and innovative channels (like job boards, social media, referrals, and talent

intelligence), tailored to fit the organization's needs and future workforce goals.

- It's important to balance efforts between active candidates (those looking for jobs) and passive ones (those not actively searching but open to opportunities).

- A source mix combines multiple sourcing methods to prevent over-reliance on one channel, which can limit diversity and increase costs.

- It's important to nurture 'near-miss' candidates to prevent talent loss. Think of this like plugging the holes in a 'leaky bucket'.

- A thoughtful sourcing strategy enables organizations to be more competitive, reduce time-to-hire, and build long-term talent pipelines that align with business goals.

REVIEW QUESTIONS

1 Why is achieving a great source mix important for organizations today?

2 What is the difference between a direct and an indirect channel?

3 Are direct or indirect channels more suitable for finding passive job seekers?

4 Describe three of the four proactive sourcing methods?

CHAPTER SEVEN

Assessment and selection

Introduction

Assessment and selection is one of the most complex and debated areas of TA. It's the most scientific part of the TA lifecycle and a critical TA building block, yet, unfortunately, it is often one of the weakest links in the recruitment process, suffering from the same difficulties as WFP. Both require a lot of input, vast amounts of data, and highly specialized skills. Many employers still rely on traditional methods, such as CV reviews, rather than leveraging more robust digital assessment tools and strategies.

This chapter will help you to understand the different approaches organizations take to assessment and selection, and the dangers of relying on traditional methods in a world where AI is taking centre stage. It will help you to understand where your own organization is in terms of assessment and selection maturity, so that you can have meaningful conversations and drive change.

In Chapter 6, we introduced the idea of the recruitment process seeming like a 'leaky bucket' with talent slipping through the cracks during the sourcing process. We take this idea further in this chapter, exploring how to guard against having a leaky bucket during the assessment and election process.

LEARNING OBJECTIVES

By the end of this chapter, you will be able to:

- Understand the foundations of assessment and selection and the importance of having a robust process in place.
- Describe some common pitfalls in the process, including a lack of objectivity and the need to overcome some typical manager responses.
- Explain different assessment methods and tools, and how to pick the right ones for your organization.
- Understand the concept of assessment validity.
- Streamline your assessment and selection process.
- Ensure fairness and reduce bias in hiring.

The importance of good assessment and selection

Assessment: An evaluation of a candidate's suitability to perform a role, using a variety of methods and stages.

Selection: The process of choosing the most suitable candidate for the role based on the assessment process, and offering them the job.

Before we look at why a good assessment and selection process is so crucial, let's first make sure we're clear about what it involves.

The process refers to the systematic approach organizations use to evaluate candidates and determine their suitability for a specific role. The goal is to ensure that the most qualified and match-fit talent is selected for each role. It typically unfolds through the following stages:

1 Screening – the process of narrowing down potential applicants from a talent pool, which typically includes manual and/or automated methods.

2 Assessment – the use of different methods to assess a candidate's suitability for a role. We delve into assessment types later in the chapter.

3 Selection – choosing the most suitable candidate for a role based on the assessment.

4 Reference checks – the process of confirming a candidate's statements and claims and verifying their skills, past performance and experience, typically with a current or former manager.

In each stage, the goal is to ensure that the most qualified and match-fit candidates are hired for each role.

Throughout the assessment and selection process, candidates are ideally objectively assessed on their behaviours, skills, competencies, strengths and cultural fit. Information is gathered from multiple sources to form a well-rounded view of their suitability for the role and organization.

Psychometrics (assessments) were first pioneered in the 19th century by Sir Francis Galton. He was a polymath fascinated by the human mind and personality and his curiosity took him to develop the world's first personality test. Galton measured physical characteristics alongside sensory and motor skills to gauge intelligence. These tests were conducted on a sample group of 17, 000 people to show that objective tests could be used to give accurate and meaningful scores. Fast forward to today, and psychometric testing has become a mainstay in hiring talent acquisition with over 75 per cent of the Time Top 100 UK companies and 80 per cent of Fortune 500 using them by 2017, particularly for graduate, technical and leadership hiring. During this time assessments have become a vital building block of TA, much like strategic workforce planning, both are key to ensuring long-term success of hiring outcomes.

Today's best-in-class organizations use psychometric testing and combine approaches such as structured interviews, online assessments, assessment centres, group exercises, and presentations. The combination of these approaches builds a complete picture of each candidate – not just their skills and experience, but their cognitive abilities, motivations, potential, and sometimes their personality, too.

> **Structured interviews:** A standardized interview process in which all candidates are asked the same questions in the same order to allow for consistent and objective comparison and evaluation.

> **Psychometric testing:** A standardized psychological assessment designed to objectively measure a candidate's cognitive abilities, personality and behavioural traits.

Common pitfalls in assessment and selection

Unfortunately, many organizations fall short of this 'best-in-class' approach.[1] Before we dive into the nitty-gritty of assessment and selection best practices, let's first consider some of the main areas where organizations can go wrong.

This is important to understand because when the wrong person is hired for a role, it can be expensive and demoralizing for everyone involved. Financially, the cost of a bad hire is often estimated to be three times their annual salary, from wasted salary, lost productivity, and training expenses to the time drained by interviews, training and onboarding.

Beyond financials, the non-monetary impacts are often even more damaging. Low morale, increased staff turnover, team burnout, and a hit to your employer brand can all follow in the wake of a poor hiring decision. Putting extra strain on an already stretched team to go through the re-hiring process can cause frustration and interview fatigue. Worst of all, if the root causes are not addressed, the same mistakes can happen again. And when the team fit isn't right? That's when friction sets in, collaboration suffers, teamwork becomes strained, and silos can start to develop, all of which will drag down the team, performance, and culture.

This ad hoc and inconsistent approach can have a serious impact on diversity and inclusion efforts – something that's often overlooked or not even realized until it's far too late. (More on equity and diversity later in the chapter.)

In Chapter 6, we considered how one of the biggest challenges in TA is ensuring talent doesn't slip through the cracks, leaving your hiring process feeling like a 'leaky bucket'. Many organizations unknowingly lose out on top candidates due to inconsistent, inefficient and/or biased selection practices. This section explores how certain behaviours, assumptions and short-term pressures in the hiring process can contribute to this talent loss.

The subjectivity trap

The subjectivity trap refers to an over-reliance on CVs, unstructured interviews and references, often without using any real assessment tools to bring objectivity to the table.

Recruitment processes can be *shockingly* subjective, with little or no structured criteria in place. Sometimes, global companies can use structured processes in one region and a completely different approach in another, all for the same talent within the same company! This kind of inconsistency creates longer-term issues that impact candidate quality, culture fit, and ultimately retention.

Hiring managers' responses to candidate selection

When under pressure, hiring managers can fall into common patterns that hinder the recruitment process, making decisions that may seem logical at the time but lead to costly mis-hires, overlooked talent, or poor team fits in the long run.

Let's break down some of the classic hiring manager responses to candidate selection. By understanding the root and hidden issues that contribute to these responses, you can navigate discussions with hiring managers and help them make more informed, strategic hiring decisions that build stronger teams and prevent high-potential and valuable candidates from slipping through the cracks.

The following are ten typical manager responses to candidate selection you are likely to have to navigate. You can use this insight to start meaningful conversations, influence decision-making, and maybe stop another 'gut hire' in its tracks:

1   **'I need the CVs. Send me all the CVs.'**
    Focus: This manager trusts traditional methods
    Root issue: They don't trust the screening process, and are over-reliant on CVs
    Problem: They'll get a limited view of candidate potential and are likely to overlook cultural fit and growth potential.

2   **'I want to rely on my intuition. I have a lot of experience.'**
    Focus: Possible bias towards background, education and experience
    Root issue: Masks diversity issues, overlooks soft skills and future potential
    Problem: Narrow view of talent, missing out on diverse perspectives and transferable skills.

3   **'Let's get this done quickly. I'm desperate and have a critical project to deliver.'**
    Focus: Time and efficiency
    Root issue: Short-staffed and under pressure
    Problem: Speed over quality, leading to potential costly mis-hires.

4   **'I'm interviewing all candidates and just have some technical questions.'**
    Focus: Time and efficiency

Root issue: Rushing the process, over-reliance on technical skills and/or domain knowledge

Problem: Misses soft skills, motivation and behavioural fit, leading to lower long-term productivity and future retention issues.

5 'I'd like a panel of three or four interviewers.'

Focus: Consistency and efficiency

Root issue: Lack of standardization, inefficiencies in decision-making

Problem: Can be overkill for entry-level roles, delays decision-making, inconsistent assessment criteria, poor candidate experience, decision fatigue with too many stakeholders.

6 'I didn't get a wow feeling.'

Focus: Trust and scepticism

Root issue: Unrealistic expectations waiting for the perfect candidate

Problem: High expectations, rejecting good candidates who could grow in-role and may match the reward offering.

7 'Let's proceed with just one round of interviews.'

Focus: Time and efficiency

Root issue: Desire to expedite the process

Problem: Risks missing key factors like cultural fit, motivation or long-term potential, and rushing into a decision without evaluation the full candidate.

8 'Let's hire someone from a similar background to our current team.'

Focus: Familiarity and comfort

Root issue: Comfort with familiar profiles

Problem: Leads to a homogenous team and limits diversity of thought and experience. Missed opportunities for innovation and creativity and will impact diversity and inclusion efforts.

9 'I don't need an assessment, I know this person, and I have a good gut feeling.'

Focus: Consistency and fairness
Root issue: Unfair process, focuses on personal bias
Problem: Can lead to subjective decisions, overlooking qualifications, soft skills and potential for growth. Impacts diversity and inclusion efforts and can also create a lack of harmony in the workforce due to perceived lack of fairness.

10 **'I don't need to do all of these online tests, I don't trust them, and I just want my *traditional human approach and process.*'**
Focus: Trust and scepticism
Root issue: Scepticism towards technology and a preference for the traditional approach.
Problem: Risk of ignoring the value of data-driven decisions; potential biases in personal judgement; limits scalability and consistency in candidate evaluation.

THE TIME, COST AND QUALITY CHALLENGE

Many hiring managers believe they can have it all: hire quickly, affordably, and with top-quality candidates. Unfortunately, this ideal is simply unachievable under normal circumstances. It may become achievable in the future through advancements in AI, but for now, real-world constraints require us to make compromises.

One of the most persistent challenges in recruitment is managing the Time, Cost and Quality challenge, as shown in Figure 7.1. Achieving a balance between these three elements is essential and understanding where to make trade-offs between them is crucial to making better hiring decisions.

Many of the typical manager responses given in the previous section suggested a focus on wanting to prioritize speed. If speed is the primary concern, candidate quality will suffer, and the hiring quality will likely be compromised. This is because rushed decisions tend to overlook critical factors like cultural fit or long-term potential.

Similarly, in the situation of a low recruitment budget when cost needs to be prioritized, both time-to-hire and the quality of

FIGURE 7.1   The time, cost and quality challenge

hire may be sacrificed. Fewer resources will make the hiring process less efficient, potentially requiring more time and effort to find quality candidates within the budget constraints.

These trade-offs are inevitable, and balancing time, cost and quality requires a clear understanding of what's most important at each stage of the recruitment process.

TOP TIP
Structure conversations using the time, cost and quality challenge

Use the time, cost and quality challenge to set realistic expectations with hiring managers. For example, if they push for a quick hire, remind them that the quality might suffer or costs could increase. Ask if they can provide you with extra budget or resource to fill a specific, time-critical campaign. Use the model to guide them towards making a more informed, balanced decision.

Choosing the right assessment methods and tools

So, how do we overcome these common hiring manager challenges? In this section, we explore assessment tools that organizations can use to make informed, data-driven decisions – decisions that will lead to better recruitment outcomes. Choosing the right assessment method is crucial because it directly impacts the quality, fairness, and effectiveness of your hiring decisions. It will improve hiring accuracy, enhance the candidate experience, save time and resources, and support data-driven decisions.

This is increasingly important to understand with over 90 per cent of young people reported to be using AI ubiquitously. Companies that are still overly reliant on CVs may find themselves dealing with candidates who have embellished or AI-enhanced their resumes. This makes a robust assessment methodology imperative.

1. Screening tools (manual and automated)

CV SCREENING (AND ITS BIASES!)

CV screening involves reviewing a candidate's CV to determine if they meet the essential requirements for a role. This process can be done manually or via technology (ATS/CRM). AI is increasingly being deployed to screen for specific keywords or criteria on a CV.

CVs are the most common tool in recruitment (it's difficult to wean hiring managers away from them), but they only offer a snapshot of *what* a person has done and they do not reveal *how* they did it, or their motivations.

CV screening can unintentionally introduce bias, even if it's unconscious. Hiring managers can make decisions based on factors such as educational pedigree, previous job titles, or even a candidate's name or location.

Gaps on a CV are another common source of bias, despite often being linked to valid life circumstances, such as maternity leave, caring responsibilities or career changes, which can be particularly relevant when considering diversity and inclusion goals.

TOP TIP
Introduce a 'blind CV' hiring strategy

Reduce unconscious bias by using a 'blind CV' hiring strategy, which removes identifying information such as name, gender, age, ethnicity or educational institution.

'Blind recruitment' takes this one step further. The CV is completely removed from the process, and candidates are assessed based on their skills and abilities. Candidates are given application questions or pre-qualifying criteria and are permitted to take online testing, rather than submitting a CV.

---

2. Online-based methods

Online-based assessments are broadly split into ability and cognitive ability tests. Both are particularly valuable for early-career or career-changer recruitment, where potential matters more than polished experience.

ABILITY TESTS

These tests evaluate specific skills or competencies that are relevant to the role, such as technical, mechanical reasoning, verbal, or numerical abilities. These tests are tailored to the role's requirements and provide insight into how well a candidate will perform specific duties and tasks. An example is a coding test for a developer or numerical reasoning for a finance role.

COGNITIVE ABILITY TESTS

Cognitive ability tests measure general mental capabilities, such as reasoning, memory, problem-solving and learning ability. These tests assess how quickly and effectively a candidate can adapt to new information or solve workplace problems. Cognitive ability tests are among the strongest predictors of job performance across a wide range of roles and industries. Common examples include IQ tests, logical reasoning tasks and puzzles. They are particularly valuable for roles that require complex problem-solving, adaptability and the ability to work with ambiguity.

PERSONALITY QUESTIONNAIRES

Personality questionnaires assess a candidate's typical behaviour, work style and potential fit within the company culture. Although they do not measure job-specific skills, they provide valuable insights into other traits, such as agility, curiosity, and relationship-building.

SITUATIONAL JUDGEMENT AND SITUATIONAL STRENGTHS TESTS

Situational judgement tests (SJTs) are designed to assess how candidates respond to real-life workplace scenarios. They explore decision-making, judgement and behavioural tendencies by asking how candidates would act in a given situation. They're especially useful in evaluating alignment with organizational values or role-specific competencies.

Situational strengths tests (SSTs) are similar in format to SJTs but take a slightly different approach. Instead of focusing on a candidate's experience or traditional competency indicators, SSTs look at a candidate's *potential* by identifying how they naturally demonstrate certain strengths. SSTs work well for roles that require no experience, and to identify long-term potential, as often candidates can demonstrate their strengths even if they have not had an opportunity to apply them in a formal work setting yet.

3. Hybrid or in-person formats

WORK SAMPLE TESTS

These simulate tasks that candidates would encounter in the role. Candidates are asked to perform tasks that replicate real-world job demands, such as drafting reports or solving problems relevant to the role. Tests such as whiteboarding exercises or hackathons are highly predictive of job performance as they replicate the actual demands of the job.

> **Whiteboarding exercise:** Candidates are given a problem (e.g. algorithm, system design, logic puzzles) and asked to give a step-by-step explanation of their solution on a whiteboard or virtual whiteboard. This is commonly used in interviews or group discussions. The candidate is invited to talk through their decision-making process, justify their choices and handle real-time interview questions to check their problem-solving skills.

> **Hackathon:** Organizations in the tech industry often hold hackathons or competitions to identify and recruit top tech talent. During the event, candidates participate in coding challenges, problem-solving tasks, or team project-related activities designed in a real-world job-simulated environment. This allows employers to see how candidates respond under pressure, collaborate and approach problems.

ASSESSMENT CENTRES

Assessment centres can involve a combination of exercises, such as role-playing, group discussions, written tasks, and case studies. These exercises are designed to evaluate how candidates perform in situations that closely resemble real work environments.

While resource-intensive, assessment centres provide a comprehensive view of a candidate's suitability for the role. They are commonly used in graduate programmes or high-volume hiring.

4. Manual (or in-person) methods

BEHAVIOURAL AND COMPETENCY INTERVIEWS

Behavioural and competency interviews focus on how candidates have handled situations in the past, assuming that past behaviour predicts future behaviour. Interviewers ask candidates to provide examples of situations where they demonstrated key competencies such as teamwork, leadership, or problem-solving.

This approach presumes candidates have prior work experience, which may disadvantage career returners, inexperienced candidates (graduates, interns, or veterans), or those without the opportunity to showcase these competencies in a traditional setting.

Many employers are now turning towards strengths-based or scenario-based interviews, which do not require past work experience. Instead, these approaches focus on identifying a candidate's potential by evaluating how they naturally demonstrate certain strengths (strengths-based), or respond to hypothetical situations (scenario-based), regardless of previous job experience. Both methods can be especially effective in evaluating early-career or career-change candidates.

STRUCTURED INTERVIEWS

All candidates are asked a consistent set of questions based on the role's key competencies. The interviewer uses standardized scoring systems to evaluate responses, ensuring fairness and minimizing bias. This method enhances the comparability of candidates and increases the validity of the hiring process.

Understanding assessment validity

There are many types of assessment listed here, and not all are equally valid, or trustworthy. It's important to ensure that we can trust our findings and be sure that we are measuring what really matters.

> **Assessment validity:** How well an assessment measures what it is intended to measure and how accurately it predicts future job performance.

According to the British Psychological Society (BPS), assessment validity refers to the extent to which a test, or any procedure used for making inferences, measures what it claims to measure, and the appropriateness of the inferences made from the test scores.[2] In simple terms, a valid assessment ensures that the tools we use in the hiring process are not only relevant but also reliable in identifying the best hires.

Establishing reliability and validity in assessment design is critical to ensure that hiring decisions are consistent, evidence-based and replicable. In short, validating and benchmarking your assessments allows you to confidently demonstrate that they meet the following key criteria:

- Predictive validity (success) – how well the assessment results can forecast a candidate's future success on the job.
- Predictive validity (failure) – how effectively the assessment rules out those unlikely to perform well.
- Fairness – how effectively the assessment avoids disadvantaging any group and supports your diversity and inclusion goals.
- Candidate experience – is the assessment acceptable and engaging enough that strong candidates are willing to complete it?

Figure 7.2 illustrates the concept of predictive validity in assessments, ranking the most common assessment tools in order of their predictive validity score. As the figure shows, assessment methods such as ability tests and structured interviews exhibit a higher predictive validity score (closer to 1) compared with more traditional approaches, such as unstructured interviews and years of experience. It highlights the importance of using structured, objective, and data-driven tools in the selection and assessment process.

Methods like ability tests and structured interviews are designed to evaluate a candidate's actual skills and behaviours in a consistent, standardized and non-biased way, ensuring that the assessment is more reliable in predicting job performance.

On the other hand, unstructured interviews lack the consistency and objectivity needed for accurate predictions. Years of experience may not always correlate with a candidate's ability to perform effectively in a new role, as it doesn't assess their motivations and other key skills that the job might need in future. Unfortunately, many hiring managers still rely on criteria such as years of experience, unstructured interviews and CVs.

KEY POINT

No assessment tool offers perfect validity. No tool or method can guarantee 100 per cent accuracy in predicting future job performance. This means that recruitment will always carry some level of risk. It's crucial to understand that while some assessments may not provide absolute certainty, they can significantly reduce hiring risk by helping to improve candidate quality and the predictability of key hiring decisions.

STOP AND THINK

Do some research into the range of assessment methods you use. Where do you sit on the scale shown in Figure 7.2?

FIGURE 7.2   The validity of different assessment methods

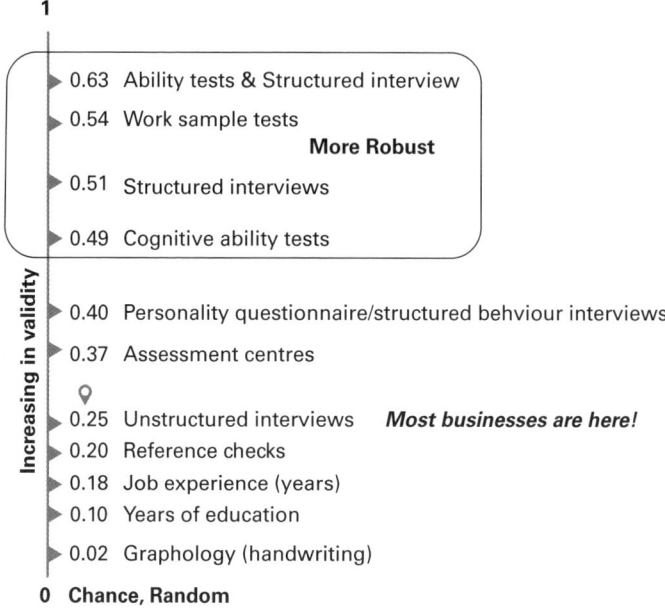

0.63   Ability tests & Structured interview

0.54   Work sample tests
                        More Robust

0.51   Structured interviews

0.49   Cognitive ability tests

0.40   Personality questionnaire/structured behviour interviews

0.37   Assessment centres

0.25   Unstructured interviews   *Most businesses are here!*

0.20   Reference checks

0.18   Job experience (years)

0.10   Years of education

0.02   Graphology (handwriting)

0   **Chance, Random**

Increasing in validity

This inherent uncertainty means that assessment will always carry a level of risk. This reality can often perpetuate the organizational trap, where stakeholders may continue to challenge best practice and the recruitment process with the central challenge: 'What's the point, it's not 100 per cent bullet proof anyway.'

Improving your assessment and selection processes

Before we delve into this section, take a look at Figure 7.3. It shows a typical assessment and selection process. Note that it does *not* represent a good process, it is simply what happens in many organizations. Two things set a great process apart from a poor one:

1 Streamlining the process.
2 Putting the candidate experience at the heart of everything.

A well-designed process eliminates unnecessary steps, removes duplication, reduces friction, and ensures candidates are treated with empathy. At the same time, the process should equip hiring managers with all the information they need to make successful, long-term hires. We will use the typical process set out in Figure 7.3 to demonstrate how many organizations can improve.

STOP AND THINK

What are your first impressions of the hiring process set out in Figure 7.3? Think about duplication, unnecessary steps and the likely candidate experience.

How to streamline your process

Streamlining a recruitment process is not about cutting corners or jeopardizing candidate quality, it's about ensuring each recruitment step adds value, aligns with objectives and enhances the candidate journey. By streamlining, we enable faster decisions, clearer communication, and a seamless flow from one stage to the next, ultimately improving both the quality of hires and the overall experience for everyone involved.

An example of what might happen in a 'poor' hiring process is when hiring managers insist on elongating it with lots of unnecessary stakeholder interviews. This can result in a broken candidate experience, unnecessary delays, and a lack of structured interviews that ultimately dilute the quality of decision-making. It not only frustrates candidates but leaves hiring teams second-guessing their choices.

FIGURE 7.3   A typical hiring process

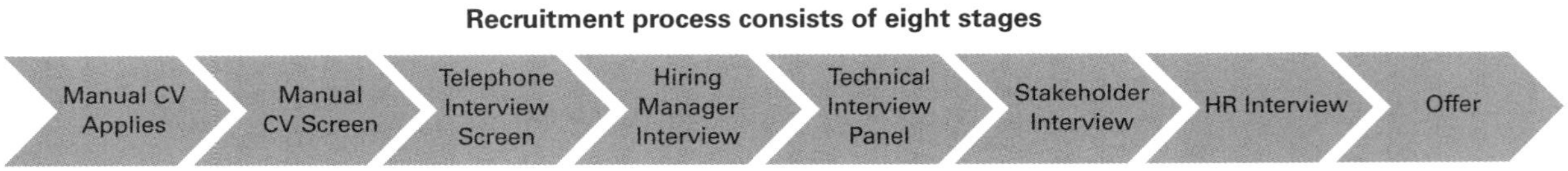

Recruitment process consists of eight stages

Manual CV Applies → Manual CV Screen → Telephone Interview Screen → Hiring Manager Interview → Technical Interview Panel → Stakeholder Interview → HR Interview → Offer

---

WHAT WOULD YOU DO?
Number 7

Your organization has already conducted two rounds of interviews with a junior candidate. Now, the hiring manager approaches you and asks for two additional stakeholders to interview the candidate for a 'sense check' before making a final decision.
　　What would you say to the hiring manager? How would you professionally challenge their request?

Addressing common process problems

Now let's look more closely at some of the problems associated with the process in Figure 7.3. You may have come up with some of these in the Stop and Think exercise.

1　**Duplication and confusion**
　　The CV or candidate has been screened twice, through a manual CV screen and a telephone interview. This could be streamlined through pre-screening questions or an online assessment tool.

2　**Too many interviews**
　　This process has too many interview stages:
　　－ Interview/telephone
　　－ Hiring manager
　　－ Stakeholder
　　－ HR
　　－ Technical
　　－ Panel
　　That's four to six rounds – excessive for most roles. It risks:
　　－ Candidate drop-off
　　－ Long time-to-hire
　　－ Inefficient use of internal time
　　－ Bias creeping in

3 **Lacks automation or efficiency**

CVs are handled manually – this suggests no automation or tech, which means:

– High administrative burden

– Risk of human bias

– Poor candidate experience (slow, unclear, inconsistent)

4 **Unclear sequencing**

Do the interviews have to appear in that order, with hiring manager first, followed by 'technical', 'stakeholder' and 'HR'? A well-structured process should have a clearly defined flow, e.g.:

– Apply

– CV Screen (automated)

– First Interview (HM)

– Final Interview (panel)

– Offer

FIGURE 7.4   Best practice recruitment process

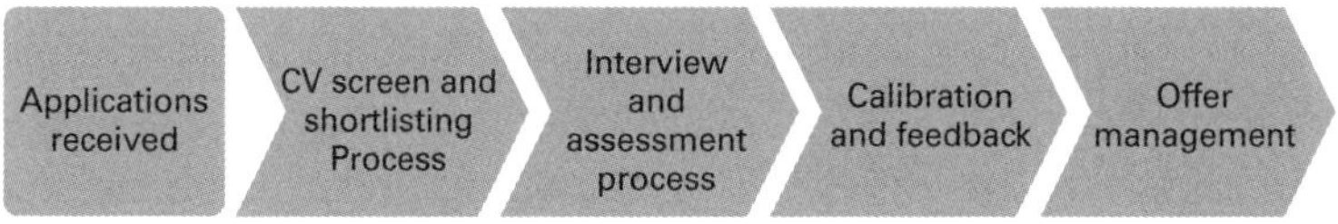

Applications received → CV screen and shortlisting Process → Interview and assessment process → Calibration and feedback → Offer management

---

STOP AND THINK

Try to gain a comprehensive understanding of how talent decisions are made in your organization. Think through the following questions:

- Does your organization lean heavily on CVs, unstructured interviews or years of experience?
    - How confident are you that these tell the full story of someone's potential?

- Do your current methods consistently lead to hiring the right quality of talent for your organization's future success?
    - Are your candidate's future match-fit? Are you hiring for fit, or for growth and capability?

- Which evidence-based methods with higher predictive validity are you not yet using?
  - Think structured interviews, skills-based assessments, job simulations, cognitive ability tests...
- Where can you shift your approach to improve fairness, consistency, and predictability in hiring decisions?
  - Are all candidates being assessed on the same criteria, in the same way?
- Could a more structured and consistent assessment approach help address diversity and inclusion gaps within your workforce?
  - Are unconscious biases creeping in?
  - How can use structure to help level the playing field?

Ensuring fairness and reducing bias in hiring

As humans, we are hardwired to make quick decisions. Every day, we subconsciously make countless decisions shaped by our innate biases. Generally, they are mental shortcuts we've built over time through our upbringing, social circles, exposure to diversity, media and lived experiences. These biases shape how we interpret the world around us, including how we assess people. And in hiring, that can lead to skewed perceptions and unfair decisions.

There are too many common cognitive biases to list in this chapter (research suggests that there are over 180 types). What matters is that we acknowledge their existence and design assessment processes that are structured, equitable and fair. The most common types in hiring are:

- Affinity bias – favouring candidates who are similar to us in background, interests or personality.
- Halo effect – letting one positive trait (a prestigious university, or employer brand) overshadow all other areas.

- Horn effect – the opposite of the halo effect, this is when one perceived negative trait clouds overall judgement (e.g. facial hair).
- Confirmation bias – looking for information that confirms our initial impression and ignoring what contradicts it.
- Name/location bias – making assumptions based on a candidate's name, address or country of origin.
- Age bias – making assumptions about someone's ability, adaptability or cultural fit based on their age; this affects both younger and older candidates.
- Nepotism bias – when personal relationships influence hiring decisions.
- Career gap bias – judging candidates negatively for time out of work, regardless of the context (e.g. caregiving, illness or study).
- Expectation anchor – a fixation on one specific piece of information about a candidate, e.g. that they must mirror the role's predecessor, or be a 'mini me' of the hiring manager. Candidates who don't match this narrow expectation are immediately discounted.

Overcoming biases such as these aren't easy, as they're often deeply ingrained through our personal life experiences. However, it's crucial that hiring managers, HR professionals, and recruiters receive adequate training to recognize these common biases. It's equally important to choose an assessment process that ensures as much objectivity as possible through structured methods helping to reduce the influence of any biases during decision-making.

WHAT WOULD YOU DO?
Number 8

A senior executive stakeholder has identified a candidate who is a close relative. The individual has not participated in the formal recruitment process but has had an informal conversation with the hiring manager. The manager now wants to offer them one of the two remaining internship roles. However, 30 candidates are currently at the assessment centre competing for those same roles.

What would you say to the hiring manager, and how would you professionally challenge their request?

Equity and equality in selection

Equality is all about giving everyone the same resources or opportunities. But it doesn't recognize that we are all unique with different circumstances and needs. That's where equity comes in. Being equitable means recognizing that not everyone starts from the same place, and adjusting resources, processes and opportunities accordingly to ensure everyone has the same chance at success. This means giving each person what they need to get an equal outcome. For example, a neurodivergent candidate may need extra time during online assessments.

This concept can be tricky for some to fully grasp, especially hiring managers who might not always pay as much attention to the finer details that a recruiter would notice!

THE EQUITY CHALLENGE IN DIGITAL ASSESSMENTS

Consider the online assessment process. On the surface, it may seem like a perfectly objective and fair way to evaluate candidates, as everyone takes the same test. But even when candidates go through the same recruitment stages, applying online through a blind process (without a CV), it is not necessarily equitable. Some demographics might be unintentionally disadvantaged, for example, depending on their socioeconomic background or schooling system. They may be more likely to suffer from assessment fatigue and drop out of the process. In these instances, equity becomes a tricky balance; what seems equal on the surface doesn't always result in an equitable process for everyone.

Recruitment teams face numerous challenges, including ensuring accessibility for diverse candidate groups and, increasingly, candidates gaming the system. The use of AI increases the risk of candidates collaborating and cheating, thereby compromising the validity of the results. This can lead to inaccurate assessments and undermine the integrity of the hiring process.

A great assessment strategy should balance online, in-person, efficiency and the candidate experience. If tests are too weighted towards automation without paying attention to the candidate experience, then there will be many dropouts, particularly by those from diverse backgrounds.

EXERCISE

Is your recruitment process truly equitable? Are all candidates in your hiring process genuinely set up to succeed, regardless of their background? Use the following four prompts to help you critically review equity in your recruitment and selection process:

1   Analyse your recruitment data. Do certain groups drop out or get filtered out at specific stages?

2   Review data by demographic (e.g. gender, ethnicity, age, disability, socioeconomic background) across your hiring funnel from application to offer. If you don't currently capture this data, start now. Implement a voluntary candidate declaration process, making it clear how the data will be used (e.g. improving fairness) and stored safely.

3   Spot the patterns. Are certain groups consistently underrepresented at later hiring stages, or not succeeding at earlier stages?

4   Review your job descriptions for bias. Job descriptions can potentially discourage some candidates. Language, tone and even formatting matter. Focus on the must-haves, strip out any jargon and ensure inclusive language is used.

CHAPTER SUMMARY

- Assessment and selection are essential components of the talent acquisition process, even though they can be frequently neglected. Many organizations have a 'leaky bucket', losing qualified candidates due to outdated, inconsistent or biased practices.

- Many organizations rely too heavily on gut instinct, CVs, unstructured interviews and lack of structured feedback calibration. This risks costly mis-hires, low retention and poor team or cultural fit.

- With the rise of AI and changing candidate expectations, robust, fair and scalable selection processes are more vital than ever.

- HR and TA must work to shift hiring mindsets, tackle bias and champion structured objective assessment tools that deliver long-term value to ensure that all hiring decisions are data-informed and aligned with the organization's goals for quality, diversity and growth.

- Common cognitive biases, like affinity bias and confirmation bias, can subtly influence hiring decisions.

- While online assessments might seem objective, they can unintentionally disadvantage candidates from underrepresented or lower socioeconomic backgrounds. Equity is about giving candidates what they need to succeed, not simply giving everyone the same.

REVIEW QUESTIONS

1 Name three typical hiring manager responses to the assessment and selection process.

2 Why does AI increase the urgency for organizations to look at their assessment and selection processes?

3 Name three biases that commonly surface during the hiring process.

Endnotes

1 HR magazine (2021) Businesses paying the financial consequences of of bad hiring, https://www.hrmagazine.co.uk/content/news/businesses-paying-the-financial-consequences-of-bad-hiring (archived at https://perma.cc/MGN9-GJXH)

2 The British Psychological Society (nd) Guidelines on testing and test use, https://www.bps.org.uk/guidelines-testing-and-test-use (archived at https://perma.cc/6YWC-5C2T)

CHAPTER EIGHT

Onboarding and retention

Introduction

In this final chapter, we look at the fifth functional TA activity building block: Onboarding and retention. Traditionally, TA's role would have terminated at this point, handing candidates over to the HR Shared Services team or the business once contracts were signed. However, onboarding, inducting and, increasingly, the ongoing development of candidates is increasingly shifting to TA.

This chapter demonstrates that TA is no longer just about hiring; it's becoming increasingly responsible for the entire talent lifecycle, having pre- and post-applicant journey oversight. Whether you work in TA or HR, this shift is important for you to understand, so you can develop the skills necessary for developing and retaining talent, as well as in acquiring talent.

This chapter shows you how to make onboarding human and intentional and use it to ignite performance. We look at the traditional process and how organizations often get it wrong, failing to create an exceptional employee experience that sets the tone for growth within the company. We look at the importance of considering employees' development as part of the onboarding process and the consequences of getting development wrong.

We then move on to what a great onboarding process looks like, considering best-in-class approaches, tips for doing it on a smaller budget and an example induction plan that you can use if you are tasked with designing one yourself.

LEARNING OBJECTIVES

By the end of this chapter, you will be able to:

- Explain the onboarding process and how it is shifting to incorporate the early development on new hires.
- Recognize the importance of prioritizing learning and development from the start of an employee's journey.
- Evaluate the long-term impact of ineffective onboarding and development practices on business success.
- Describe what a good pre- and onboarding process looks like for early careers, professional and executive hiring.
- Design a structured, inclusive induction and apply the knowledge to your own organization.

What is onboarding?

Onboarding is the final stage in the TA lifecycle. It involves welcoming new employees into the company, ensuring that they understand their role, their fit within the broader company and the organization's culture, values and processes.

Traditionally, there are four main stages, which organizations do to varying degrees:

1 Pre-boarding – the time between when someone is offered a role and their first day as an employee.
2 Induction – begins on day one of someone's employment and typically lasts for a few hours or days. This is a short-term process that equips employees with everything they need to get started in their roles.

3 Training – happens over a longer timeframe than orientation and equips employees with specific knowledge and skills they need to perform their roles well.

4 Ongoing support – regular check-ins to get feedback from the employee and ensure they are adjusting to the role well.

Ideally, onboarding should be a launchpad into a company's culture, purpose and vision.

Problems with traditional onboarding

Onboarding is more than just paperwork; it's your brand in motion and the launchpad into a company's culture, purpose and vision. It is the first real impression a new hire gets of a company beyond the recruitment process, and getting it right matters. A person's experience of a company from the moment they accept a job offer is vital for shaping their future success in the role.

Yet, all too often, onboarding – the very launchpad into an organization's culture, purpose and values – is often under-invested, and is viewed primarily as a compliance exercise. Instead of being seen as a critical moment to engage and empower new hires, setting the tone for growth, connection and performance, it's reduced to a checklist of paperwork, policy briefings and mandatory training modules.

Onboarding often falls solely within the remit of Learning and Development (L&D) staff, who, while crucial to the learning process, aren't always plugged into the hiring experience and the initial talent profiling. They may lack a broader understanding of candidate quality at a high level, as well as specific insights into the candidates' specific strengths and talent needs or skills gaps at an individual level.

This kind of onboarding experience is a missed chance to spark belonging, build momentum and lay the foundations for long-term success. According to Gallup, only 12 per cent of employees agree that their organization has a good onboarding process.[1] The following are some important employee onboarding facts that every HR professional needs to know:

- Onboarding improves new hire retention by 82 per cent, and productivity by over 70 per cent.[2]
- Structured onboarding brings a 60 per cent year-on-year improvement in revenue.[3]
- New employees with good onboarding experiences are 18 times more committed to their employer.
- 58 per cent of organizations say that their onboarding programme is focused on processes and paperwork.[4]

In Chapter 7, we considered the cost of a bad hire. The cost of a poor post-hire experience is the same. New hires need the right foundations and support. Without it, even the most talented individuals can fail to reach their potential in the company. Despite the clear link between onboarding, performance and productivity, many organizations fail to treat onboarding as a core building block of TA and talent development. Much like workforce planning – the starting point of TA – onboarding represents the final bookend.

STOP AND THINK

Think back to your own onboarding. Did it make you feel connected to the company's vision and culture? Or did it feel uninspiring, with little alignment to what you actually needed to succeed? Did it equip you with the tools, relationships, and knowledge to make an impact from day one – or leave you feeling like you were catching up from the start?
   This is referred to as the onboarding blind spot.

Reframing onboarding as development

This chapter is not just called 'Onboarding'. It's called 'Onboarding and retention'. The fifth TA building block brings these two elements together as we find that TA is increasingly becoming responsible for early candidate engagement, development and retention.

Modern TA is reframing the final stage of the TA lifecycle not just as onboarding, but as the beginning of an employee's development journey within an organization. Where the worlds of talent acquisition and development meet is where the magic happens. It's in that intersection that organizations don't just make successful hires – they nurture thriving, high-impact employees from day one. Effective onboarding bridges the gap between recruitment and retention. Dropping the baton at this stage can affect employer brand, engagement and productivity.

This transition towards TA becoming responsible for onboarding and retention makes sense for many reasons:

- It completes the candidate experience – as we have seen throughout this book, TA owns the rest of the lifecycle. If onboarding isn't aligned with the EVP and candidate attraction, the experience will feel disjointed and lack authenticity for new hires.
- TA sits at the intersection between two of the most critical 'customers' for the organization – candidates and hiring managers. No other function has this unique, real-time view of relationships, expectations, experience, and delivery. TA understands why certain skills were prioritized in the hiring plans, the specific talent the organization needs and the support new hires will require to thrive.
- TA also owns critical talent data on hiring trends, candidate pipelines, skill gaps, and market dynamics. These insights are important to better hiring, and are foundational to early development planning, workforce forecasting, and even informing internal mobility and retention strategies.
- Onboarding can affect the early performance experience of an employee, their time to productivity and retention – all key metrics that TA should track.
- Increasingly, TA functions have the capacity to take on talent development as AI removes more and more routine tasks. The function is being liberated from administration and freed

up to be more strategic, looking further downstream at hiring efficiency impact.

For these reasons, TA is increasingly responsible for onboarding and not stepping away and handing onboarding over to L&D teams, leaving a gap where no one truly owns the end-to-end experience. TA is staying involved. This provides organizations with the opportunity to give an exceptional employee experience, starting from the moment someone is offered a job.

What happens when talent isn't developed?

So many hires fail to reach their full potential. This section explores the key challenges organizations face after selecting individuals who seem to fit the role, yet struggle to develop them into people who can truly thrive and succeed within it.

One of the main issues at the heart of this challenge is the ongoing talent shortage – an issue that's only growing, especially with the current challenge of an 'ageing' workforce, with the largest proportion of the workforce reaching retirement age. The skills gap continues to widen, while digitalization and the automation of work through AI are creating even more shifts in the skills landscape. Organizations are facing a perfect storm of capability loss and skill misalignment. In short, skills now have a shelf life, and it's getting shorter.

Against this backdrop, onboarding is now more important than ever to kick-start development from day one with a thoughtful onboarding experience that combines continuous learning and clear, structured development pathways. A poor onboarding experience leads to missed growth opportunities, not only jeopardizing the individual's performance, but also undermining long-term organizational goals. Ultimately, it can lead to unplanned attrition.

Attrition: The gradual reduction in the number of employees in an organization over time, typically due to:

- Resignations.
- Retirements.
- Deaths.
- Involuntary separations (e.g. redundancies or dismissals).

Attrition can be voluntary and involuntary.

Voluntary attrition: When employees choose to leave the organization, for example, a resignation for a new job, retirement or for personal/family reasons. It often reflects employee dissatisfaction, better external opportunities, or life changes. Organizations may analyse this to improve retention, benefits, or workplace culture.

Involuntary attrition: When the employer initiates the separation, for example, layoffs due to restructuring, cost-cutting, downsizing or termination for poor performance or misconduct. It may be part of strategic workforce planning or result from external pressures. It can impact morale and employer reputation if not handled carefully.

Prioritizing learning and development from the start

To address these issues, L&D must be a central focus for TA and HR teams. The requirement for reskilling and upskilling has never been more important, not just to bridge the skills gap but to ensure long-term success. Intentional strategies that are integrated into onboarding help create a learning culture and build skills faster. This also helps to retain employees.

This is why it's becoming crucial for the HR and TA functions to collaborate and align with the broader business strategy, fostering a people-centric culture that integrates learning, growth, and engagement across the workforce. Talent needs to lead business strategy and should be nurtured and recognized as the key contributor to competitive advantage.

EXERCISE

Think about your own organization's current onboarding process.

Step 1: Map the current journey

- When does onboarding officially start?
- Who is involved in each stage?
- What does the pre-boarding period include (if anything)?

Step 2: Identify ownership and gaps

- Who owns each part of the process (TA, L&D, line manager, HRBP)?
- Are there any handover points?
- Where do you notice delays, duplication or disengagement?

What does a good onboarding process look like?

So, what is the definition of a great onboarding experience? Onboarding should begin well before the new hire's start date – ideally at the offer stage. A well-honed pre-boarding experience should be in place to keep hires engaged and connected to the company.

We'll consider preboarding and onboarding through the lens of 'hiring type'. There are three different types of hires: early career, professional hiring and executive hiring. The timeframes, focus areas and strategies for pre-boarding and onboarding differ for each hiring type, depending on the nature of the role and expectation. We'll consider these now.

> **Early career:** Entry-level or graduate hires, typically with limited work experience.

> **Professional hiring:** Experienced individuals with specific skills and industry knowledge.

> **Executive hiring:** Senior leaders or C-suite roles (e.g. CEO, CFO, CTO).

Early careers

PRE-BOARDING FOCUS:

- Strong TA focus to reduce reneging and keep students engaged before critical intake points of the year.
- Offer holder events.
- Pre-boarding activities to maintain interest and spark commitment.

LONGER PRE-BOARDING TIMELINE:

- From 6 to 12 months due to cyclical recruitment and academic schedules, with a focus on engagement and retention.

ONBOARDING FOCUS:

- Mentorship and buddy systems.
- Cultural immersion.
- Structured learning programmes.
- Rotation development programmes to provide exposure to different business units.

Professional hiring

PRE-BOARDING FOCUS:

- Typically has minimal TA focus and activities, primarily regular check-ins to ensure compliance with start dates and paperwork.
- Focus on confirming role expectations and readiness.

PRE-BOARDING TIMELINE:

- Two to three months due to less complex timelines and quicker integration requirements.

ONBOARDING FOCUS:

- Immediate role-specific training and team integration.
- Focus on key skills and early performance milestones.
- Clear alignment on goals and expectations for the first 90 days.

Executive hiring

PRE-BOARDING FOCUS:

- High-touch, personalized engagement, including personal calls.
- Engagement with senior leadership to help build loyalty and commitment.

LONGER PRE-BOARDING TIMELINE:

- From 6 to 12 months due to extended notice periods and garden leave requirements.

ONBOARDING FOCUS:

- Executive onboarding sessions, focusing on strategic vision and leadership alignment.

- Focus on cross-functional introductions and relationship building.
- Focus on integrating into the broader company strategy and vision.

Forward-thinking employers blend some of the best practices from both early careers and executive hiring into the professional hiring process. Professional hiring often feels lighter in comparison, even though the bulk of hiring typically occurs at this level. By adopting elements from early careers, such as mentorship programmes and structured engagement, alongside the high-touch approach seen in executive hiring, organizations could create a more comprehensive and impactful experience for professional hires. This would help improve integration, reduce turnover, and accelerate time to productivity.

EXERCISE

Think about your own organization's current pre- and onboarding process for professional hiring. Are there any areas where elements of the early careers or executive practices outlined earlier could be adapted to strengthen the onboarding journey? For example:

- Could a mentor or buddy be introduced?
- Is there any communication or cultural immersion missing in pre-boarding?
- What simple win could you suggest?

TOP TIP
Collaborate to identify gaps

Running a collaborative workshop with L&D, Talent, and HR to map the onboarding journey will save time, foster alignment, and provide a proactive approach for identifying duplication, gaps, and areas for improvement. You can even use free tools, like Mural, Miro, Trello, Canva, Google Jamboard, to make the process more interactive and engaging.

Best-in-class onboarding experiences

Companies that offer best-in-class onboarding foster a sense of belonging and align the experience with their EVP, culture and values. Large companies with big budgets can leverage technology to offer personalized experiences to new recruits. For example, new hires can receive tailored content based on their role, location and business area. They can be sent reminders, be encouraged to connect with colleagues early and be guided through key learning checkpoints that drive fast productivity. Some organizations enhance onboarding by offering personalized welcome kits with company swag and celebrating cultural events like birthdays and Easter.

However, you don't have to have a big budget to deliver a thoughtful and connected onboarding experience; you just need purpose, coordination, and a bit of creativity. The core principles are the same if you work in a smaller company with a comparatively small budget. Consider if you can suggest any of the following for your organization. You might be able to significantly enhance the onboarding experience:

- **Personalization**: Foster a welcoming culture by sending personalized emails or a letter from the CEO or leadership, outlining the company's values and excitement about investing in new talent. Use templated emails, intro videos from managers, and role-specific FAQs to make new hires feel seen and valued.
- **Leverage free tools**: Harness free resources like Google Forms for feedback, Canva or PowerPoint for visual welcome packs, and Slack, Jamboard, or Miro for collaborative team introductions.

- **Promote interactive culture building**: Organize team-building activities, or events/socials, whether virtual coffee chats, team lunches, or casual Zoom meetups, that help new hires connect with colleagues in a relaxed setting.
- **Create a shared communication hub**: Set up a dedicated channel on Slack or MS Teams where new hires can interact with peers, share tips, and celebrate milestones together.
- **Involve real people**: Assign a buddy or mentor – either a peer or their manager – to guide new hires through the first few weeks. Help them schedule intro coffee chats and encourage team-wide welcome messages.
- **Offer a structured, clear agenda**: Provide a simple first-day induction plan or an agenda for the first week. A clear timeline, even without advanced tech, with meetings, intros, and learning milestones, helps new hires feel grounded.
- **Build a feedback loop**: Keep the momentum going with pre-start check-ins and post-start surveys. These show you care while allowing you to continuously refine and improve the onboarding process.

TOP TIP
CEO letter for employee engagement

Consider sending a welcome letter from your CEO as part of the pre-boarding process. This simple yet impactful gesture not only makes new hires feel valued but showcases the company's commitment to building a personal connection. And, if word gets out that you do this, it can strengthen the employer brand. It's super easy to do, and highly impactful!

A closer look at the induction

Whether crammed into a single day or stretched over two or three, inductions often result in confusion and fatigue. They are a missed opportunity to spark excitement and a genuine sense of belonging from day one. They usually involve sitting (remotely) through a tick-box exercise and enduring a full day of codes of conduct, E-learning completions, GDPR modules, IT setup (if you're lucky), sickness reporting, fraud awareness, anti-bribery, diversity policies... and maybe a brief overview of the company thrown in. It doesn't matter whether the organization is big or small; the experience is often the same.

Designing a good induction

Induction design needs to be intentional, with the candidate experience at its heart. Of course, the process needs to meet compliance requirements, but that doesn't mean all the energy and excitement have to be drained out of it.

The following are some great induction elements that you could consider for your induction experience. Any of these will help you to focus on designing an experience around people, not internal processes and compliance and that builds excitement about the company:

· Assigning a buddy and mentor to the new hire.
· The company's 'why' is built in; its purpose and CSR.
· Leadership talks are included, where they discuss their journeys and challenges.
· Includes real stories and lived experiences.
· Incorporates human connection and peer-to-peer networking.
· Presents an inspiring vision to create a sense of belonging.
· Opportunity to sign up for diversity networks.

An example of an induction plan

The boxed induction plan places minimal emphasis on policy or compliance-related content. Rather than front-loading with technical information, consider how you can prioritize connection and culture so that new recruits can begin their journey with a sense of purpose and belonging.

The structure draws inspiration from best practices within graduate hiring and high-volume professional intake programmes, where scalable, repeatable touchpoints have the greatest impact. While designed with interns in mind, many of the concepts can be flexed to suit other early careers pathways or broader talent acquisition programmes, such as professional hiring.

The schedule can also be easily converted into a virtual format with careful planning and thoughtful execution. To ensure as engaging an experience as possible, incorporate team breakouts in Microsoft Teams or Zoom, clear session parameters, and interactive elements. Real-time feedback polls, the use of emojis for feedback loops, and other digital tools can help foster interaction and keep the energy up throughout the day. By leveraging virtual collaboration platforms effectively, you can maintain an engaging, inclusive, and fun environment, even remotely.

EXAMPLE
Induction plan for graduate hiring/interns

- Welcome and kick-off: 09:00 – 09:45
  Meet the early careers team, get an overview of the day and break the ice with a fun activity.

- Discovering who we are: 09:45 – 10:15
  Hear from senior leaders as they share what makes this company unique – our mission, values and the impact you'll help create from day one.

- Culture and connections: 10:15 – 11:00
  Learn about employee networks, clubs and initiatives that make our culture inclusive, collaborative and future-focused. Information on how you can get involved.

- Coffee break: 11:00 – 11:15
  Time to recharge, grab a drink and prepare for the next session.

- Explore the workplace: 11:15 – 12:00
  Explore the physical or virtual workspace. Meet immediate team members. Opportunity for a team photo.

- Inclusion and belonging: 12:00 – 12:30
  Hear real-world stories from our current graduates and their personal insights and impactful moments in our special DE&I spotlight session.

- Lunch with the team: 12:30 – 13:15
  Enjoy lunch with peers and mentors.

- People and policies: 13:15 – 14:15
  HR will walk you through key policies, support tools and benefits to make sure you're set up for success.

- Your role and integration: 14:15 – 15:00
  Dive into your team's goals and projects, meet your buddy or mentor and get an idea of what your day-to-day will look like.

- Short break: 15:00 – 15:15
  A little break before we wrap up.

- Q&A and social networking: 15:15 – 16:00
  Tools like Kahoot, Mentimeter or Slido. Join a relaxed fireside chat session to ask questions via our quiz, share reflections and take part in speed networking.

- Vision and voice: 16:00 – 16:30
  An uplifting close to the day. Hear from a recent intern or early career professional who has progressed in the company.

- Wrap-up and what's next: 16:30
  Key takeaways and what's coming up in your first week.

TOP TIP
Design an inclusive experience

Think about ways to make your induction experience inclusive. For example, neurodivergent intakes, especially those with conditions like autism or ADHD, may experience heightened stress or anxiety when faced with ambiguity. Starting a new role can be overwhelming, so provide as much clarity and structure as you can, reducing surprises by clearly outlining each step in advance.

EXERCISE

How can you enhance your induction process to help new hires feel engaged, included and set up for success? Use the following questions to help guide your thinking:

1 What does a great induction experience look like to you?
   – Think about emotional impact, culture, clarity – not just logistics.

2 What are the three most important things a new hire should feel by the end of their induction (e.g. connected, confident, curious)?

3 What works well in your current induction process?
   – Is it striking the right balance, or is it overly focused on compliance?
   – Have you created 'moments of delight' to welcome new hires in a meaningful way?

4 What feedback is available from recent starters, hiring managers or mentors?
   – What can we learn from their past experiences?

5 What do you need to:
   – Stop doing?
   – Start doing?
   – Continue doing?
   – Move to a new format (e.g. in-person to digital)?

Action planning

1 Who do you need to involve to bring about change?

2 How will you measure if the induction experience is improving? (Surveys, stay interviews, attrition data, pulse checks?)

TOP TIP
How to build an experience with a small budget?

1 Start early – engagement begins the moment an offer is accepted. Pre-welcome communications can create a sense of belonging?

2 Prioritize people over policy – move beyond compliance and heavy PowerPoint presentations; build an experience that focuses on human connection.

3 Design for inclusion – the experience should be inclusive, interactive and scalable with clear agendas and breakout sessions (whether in-person or virtual).

CHAPTER SUMMARY

- Onboarding is not just the end of recruitment. It is the beginning of talent development. A successful recruitment journey should focus on long-term growth.

- Collaborate with learning teams to ensure onboarding is a seamless, strategic hand-up, not a mere handover.

- As an HR or TA professional, it's essential to balance the traditional, compliance-heavy approach with a fresh, people-first strategy.

- Engagement begins the moment the offer is accepted. Pre-welcome communications help ease anxiety, set expectations and promote a sense of belonging. This is particularly important for neurodivergent hires.

- Onboarding doesn't have to be costly or overly complicated. A great experience can be delivered with minimal frills.

- Design an inclusive induction programme that fosters engagement, builds belonging, and sets new hires up for long-term success.

REVIEW QUESTIONS

1 What are the four stages of the onboarding process?

2 Why is it important to collaborate with L&D when designing the onboarding process?

3 Name three ways to provide a best-in-class induction on a budget.

4 How can you design an induction experience with neurodivergent hires in mind?

Endnotes

1 Gallup (nd) Why the onboarding experience is key for retention, https://www.gallup.com/workplace/235121/why-onboarding-experience-key-retention.aspx (archived at https://perma.cc/A95Y-CM7C)

2 Cooke, M (2022) The great onboarding: How social and collaborative learning can create rapid alignment, Brandon Hall Group, 28 April, https://brandonhall.com/the-great-onboarding-how-social-and-collaborative-learning-can-create-rapid-alignment (archived at https://perma.cc/RR8M-BFYG)

3 Mulcahy, S (nd) Avoiding the high cost of poor onboarding, Enboarder, https://enboarder.com/blog/poor-onboarding/#:~:text=Other%20research%20by%20Northpass%20highlighted%20that%20businesses,onboarding%20saw%20a%2060%20increase%20in%20revenue (archived at https://perma.cc/AQJ9-EU5J)

4 Oak Engage (2025) 24 shocking employee onboarding statistics you need to know in 2024, 10 April, https://www.oak.com/blog/employee-onboarding-statistics (archived at https://perma.cc/S58M-LMSD)

Conclusion

This book has sought to introduce TA to early career HR and TA professionals. It has provided a strategic and practical framework of recruitment, highlighting key challenges, best practices and opportunities for the profession as a whole, as well as for you individually at the start of your career.

This concluding chapter focuses on the future – both your future and the future of TA. It provides further guidance on how you can grow into a Talent Value Leader in a profession that is being reshaped by AI. While this innovation offers exciting opportunities to remove routine-based tasks, elevate the candidate experience and drive more strategic hiring decisions, it also brings a new set of complex ethical, legal and reputational risks which will require you to develop the right mindset and skills to navigate. This concluding chapter returns to the taxonomy of TA skills introduced in Chapter 2. Reflect on your current strengths and development areas as you work through the chapter, keeping in mind your organization's culture and your desired future career direction.

It's exciting that HR now stands at the precipice of a technological breakthrough that will impact people. The change is unprecedented. HR is at a pivotal crossroads, uniquely positioned to evolve into true talent-value leaders, with a transformative opportunity to lead this change across the workforce. The future of TA will not just be about technology; it will be about people with the right skills to shape technology solutions that solve the right business problems.

It's time for HR and TA to step up and grow into true talent value leaders, rather than standing by passively as AI takes hold of organizations without human-centered considerations.

> **LEARNING OBJECTIVES**
>
> By the end of this chapter, you will be able to:
> - Explain how AI is likely to impact the future of TA and your career.
> - Review and reflect on your skills and mindset in TA.
> - Consolidate your learning from this book.
> - Develop an action plan for influencing recruitment strategy in your organization.

AI and the future of TA

AI offers tremendous potential to transform recruitment, but only if it is applied thoughtfully and ethically.

The future of recruitment will demand HR and TA professionals to develop a new mindset and new skills. But by mastering the real-world, day-to-day implications of AI in recruitment, you'll be able to not just navigate the future but shape it, moving away from low-value administrative tasks. The role HR plays in guiding the responsible adoption of AI in recruitment is becoming increasingly critical. By understanding this, you'll position yourself as a trusted advisor, championing fairness, inclusivity and human oversight at every stage of the TA lifecycle.

As noted in the *Harvard Business Review* article 'Transforming talent acquisition through the power of automation and artificial intelligence',[1] HR teams have long been overburdened with repetitive, manual tasks – often operating within outdated systems that have seen little innovation since the early 2000s. The arrival of AI is reshaping that landscape. Automation is now handling tasks like interview scheduling in real time, freeing recruiters to focus on more strategic conversations with candidates and hiring managers – conversations that tackle the bigger challenges at play.

Countless new AI solutions are emerging on the market that are designed to streamline recruitment processes and increase efficiency. They include CV scanning and AI-powered chatbots to facilitate real-time candidate interactions. AI is poised to not only augment the candidate experience, from the initial application through to onboarding, but also enable companies to measure engagement, tenure, commitment, and performance. AI may even be able to potentially predict events like another Great Resignation.

However, AI is not intended to replace recruiters, but to help amplify their capabilities. The automation of tasks like CV screening, for instance, will theoretically free up TA teams to focus on more strategic aspects of recruitment. Generative AI (GenAI) is signalling an exciting shift in this approach.

Imagine a future where CVs are a relic of the past. Instead of relying on paper or digital CVs, AI could evaluate candidates by observing their performance in simulated work environments. Imagine using virtual reality (VR) interviews that assess problem-solving skills through interactive tasks, producing data based on real-world skills rather than traditional methods. AI could also match candidates to jobs more efficiently, follow up on incomplete applications, and nurture passive talents. AI is set to transform how talent is sourced, engaged, and retained in the future.

As recruitment continues to evolve with AI, it will be the role of HR to critically evaluate how future innovations will impact fairness and equity in hiring.

Technology shortcomings hamper progress

According to the *Harvard Business Review*, while many organizations are eager to adopt AI, only 26 per cent have modernized their TA technology stack.

It's clear that technology plays an essential role in talent acquisition (notably one of the TA building blocks), yet only 44 per cent of companies are satisfied with the tools they currently use, as outdated legacy systems fall short of their promised innovations. Automation adoption is also lagging, with only 52 per cent of respondents reporting that their organization has automated some steps or areas of the TA process, while 37 per cent have yet to automate anything.

The reasons behind the slow adoption of automation are different. Respondents point to factors such as the high cost of automation technologies (38 per cent), the lack of digital expertise and mindset among recruitment and HR leadership (33 per cent), difficulty justifying the ROI of TA automation (33 per cent), uncertainty around the best technologies for automation (32 per cent), and a lack of prioritization of TA automation by leadership (30 per cent). These results highlight that there is no clear consensus on how to effectively drive TA automation as a priority.

Organizations that cultivate digital expertise within HR and recruitment leadership and prioritize AI adoption and emerging technologies will emerge as the talent acquisition leaders of the future.

According to a new report by the Business Research Company, AI in the HR market is to skyrocket to $14.08 billion by 2029.[2]

AI driven tools will continue to revolutionize how we work in recruitment by automating repetitive tasks by 74 per cent, speeding up candidate sourcing by 67 per cent, and enhancing candidate engagement by 59 per cent.

Navigating this ambiguity calls for a new kind of HR and TA mindset – one grounded in adaptability, open thinking and, above all, resilience and curiosity. That, more than any tool or technology, is the skill that will shape the future of HR and most importantly, your future. The role that HR plays in guiding the responsible adoption of AI in recruitment is becoming increasingly critical.

How AI will shape your career in TA and/or HR

As an early career professional, you are in a unique position to influence and shape the future of TA within your organization. As you begin your HR and/or TA journey, it's essential to understand the transformative role AI will play in TA and how you can embrace this change.

AI-powered tools are set to revolutionize how HR and recruitment professionals streamline hiring processes, improve candidate engagement, and make data-driven decisions. But AI's influence goes beyond technology; it will shape how you approach your career in HR. As we covered in Chapter 1, you'll need to balance AI's efficiency with the human touch that makes recruitment truly successful. Use the exercise below to think about how your organization can preserve the human essence of hiring while embracing the opportunities that technology brings.

The future of hiring may well look very different from the hiring processes that we know today. At the same time, as companies integrate more AI into their hiring processes, transparency over its usage becomes critical. Candidates want to know how AI is being used in the process, why it's being used, and how decisions are being made. A lack of clarity can lead to mistrust or scepticism, which in turn can damage your employer brand.

It's more important than ever to think about the future challenges and how technology is thoughtfully used. By staying curious (as we highlighted earlier in the taxonomy of the future of TA and HR skills), future-focused and committed to the human side of hiring, you'll be well-positioned to lead in this new era of recruitment.

STOP AND THINK

Reflect on the following questions to help stay ahead of the curve and shape more inclusive, future-ready hiring strategies:

- What would a hiring process without traditional resumes look like in your organization? How might it support more equitable and skills-based hiring?

- How will candidates be evaluated in future through dynamic skills assessments?

- How transparent is your company about the role AI plays in hiring decisions?

- How does this transparency (or lack of it) shape candidate perceptions and influence your employer brand?

- What steps can you take to ensure technology is being used ethically, inclusively, and in alignment with your company's values?

EXERCISE

Reflect on how your organization is navigating the balance between technology innovation and human connection in recruitment using the following prompts:

1 **Using technology thoughtfully**
How can you ensure that AI enhances, not replaces, the human connection in recruitment?

2 **Optimizing the candidate experience**
What steps can you take to ensure technology supports a seamless, authentic and fair candidate journey and experience?

3 **Ensuring authentic responses**
    How does your organization ensure it has authentic candidate
    responses, rather than AI-assisted assessments? How can
    your organization validate the authentic representation of its
    potential?

4 **Balancing automation with human interaction**
    What elements of recruitment should be automated and what
    should be human-centred? Think about the balance between
    building trust, the recruitment experience, engagement and
    employer brand.

5 **Exploring new possibilities**
    If your company hasn't yet started incorporating AI into
    recruitment, where might you recommend exploring potential
    solutions given the earlier insights from this chapter? How
    could you provide insights or examples to help your business
    tentatively start the journey?

Applying the TA skills taxonomy

As TA continues to evolve, tomorrow's HR professionals must
develop certain key strengths and a curious mindset to stay
ahead of emerging trends. Chapter 2 introduced the TA skills
taxonomy to help you become a strategic talent partner and
develop the right mindset to succeed in the AI-driven world. As
a reminder, there are five foundational strengths essential to
transforming TA into a strategic business partnership. They
represent the knowledge and capability necessary to drive meaningful change and transform yourself into a true talent value
partner. These strengths are:

1. Data fluency

This is a core capability, central to decision-making in TA. This
is not just about reading reports but interpreting, translating,

and applying hiring data to shape strategic hiring decisions. This includes transforming raw metrics into actionable insights. In a recruitment intake meeting, for example, a data-fluent HR professional could use the following to guide hiring managers towards realistic expectations and smarter recruitment strategies:

- External market intelligence (competitor insights).
- Internal benchmarks (time to hire or cost per hire).

Data fluency enables professionals to predict hiring needs, assess candidate quality and optimize sourcing strategies.

2. Global mindset

This is the ability to approach TA with a broad, inclusive, and informed perspective that understands and adapts to different regional cultures, labour laws, and market trends. A global mindset is critical when recruiting across regions with diverse market conditions. It helps HR teams navigate:

- Cross-border hiring challenges.
- Regional skill shortages.
- Cultural nuances in candidate engagement.

For instance, in a recruitment update meeting, you might highlight talent shortages in a specific location and guide the business to invest in a longer-term graduate talent strategy, or establish a strategic hub in a location with stronger talent pipelines.

3. Digital agility

Digital agility refers to the ability to confidently use and integrate digital tools, platforms, and technologies to enhance, simplify, and scale the TA lifecycle. This includes everything from workflow automation to leveraging AI, analytics, and digital candidate engagement strategies. It's about tech-enabled thinking that empowers smarter, faster and more human-centred recruiting. Digital agility means being able to:

- Navigate AI-driven recruitment platforms for candidate screening or sourcing.
- Use tools like Power BI to measure the ROI of recruitment channels or diversity outcomes.
- Automate administrative tasks (e.g. interview scheduling, candidate communication) to streamline hiring.
- Run digital campaigns via social media, CRM tools, or programmatic job advertising to attract talent.
- Design seamless digital candidate experiences from application to onboarding.

4. Commerciality

Commerciality refers to having a deep understanding of how the business operates, makes money, and achieves its strategic goals, combined with the ability to align TA strategies to drive commercial outcomes. TA is no longer just a back-office function, it's a strategic enabler of growth. Commerciality means:

- Knowing the cost of unfilled roles – every empty seat means lost productivity, missed revenue, or delayed delivery.
- Making ROI-driven decisions – choosing sourcing strategies that balance cost and quality.
- Prioritizing roles that impact the bottom line – understanding which hires are critical for revenue, growth, or transformation.
- Communicating in business terms – translating TA metrics into commercial impact (e.g. cost impact on customer delivery, revenue enablement).
- Lastly, building compelling business cases, crafting evidence-based proposals to justify strategic hiring decisions.

5. Creativity

Creativity is the ability to innovate and design new ways to attract, engage and retain top talent, especially in a landscape where processes are increasingly automated and standardized.

As AI becomes the great leveller, optimizing and streamlining recruitment for everyone, employers risk blending in and not 'standing out'. Creativity is what allows TA teams to break that mould and build emotional, memorable, and authentic talent connections. A creative TA function can:

- Develop standout employer branding that resonates in a crowded digital space.
- Craft unique sourcing campaigns that go beyond LinkedIn and job boards.
- Deliver personalized candidate experiences that feel more human, not automated.
- Build compelling storytelling into recruitment marketing.
- Design new pipelines and programmes (returnships, early talent campaigns) in overlooked talent areas.

Creativity is about strategic problem-solving that helps your organization stand out and stay relevant in a competitive hiring landscape.

Reviewing your skills, knowledge and mindset

The 'review questions' at the end of each chapter can help you assess your understanding of the subjects discussed throughout this book. To further help you assess your skills, knowledge and mindset against the TA skills taxonomy, you may find it useful to undertake the assessment exercise in the box.

EXERCISE
Skills, knowledge and mindset assessment – talent acquisition

Ask yourself the following questions:

Strategic mindset
- Do you recognize that talent drives business strategy, not the other way around?

- Have you strengthened your understanding that HR and TA must influence business direction, not just react to it?
- Can you clearly describe the key TA functional building blocks and give examples of best practice in each?

Global mindset – knowledge

- Do you regularly consider regional labour market trends and cultural expectations in your hiring strategies?
- Have you ever helped to adapt a talent strategy based on local skills shortages, supply and demand of skills, or cultural nuance?
- Can you confidently guide the business on cross-border hiring challenges or opportunities?
- Do you understand labour laws in your current operating countries where you recruit?
- Have you suggested or implemented location-based hiring strategies, like graduate programmes or talent hubs, to bridge skills shortages?

Global mindset – skills

- Have you developed cultural intelligence and sensitivity?
- Do you know about international labour markets and employment laws?
- Are you curious about strategic workforce planning across regions?

Global mindset – behaviour

- Do you demonstrate curiosity and openness to other cultures?
- Do you adapt recruitment practices to suit local norms?
- Do you seek diverse perspectives and values inclusion?
- Do you use data to anticipate regional hiring challenges and stakeholder needs?

Digital fluency – knowledge

- Are you confident using digital tools (e.g. ATS, CRM, AI sourcing tools or Boolean search strings to source on different platforms proactively) to enhance the recruitment process?

- Do you use data analytics (e.g. Power BI or other dashboards) to assess the effectiveness of hiring strategies?
- Have you automated or streamlined any part of the recruitment workflow recently?
- Do you support the execution of digital campaigns to attract specific talent pools?
- How seamless is the digital experience you offer candidates, from application to onboarding?

Digital fluency – skills

- How proficient are you with recruitment technology (ATS, CRM, AI sourcing tools, etc.)?
- How data literate are you (e.g. using dashboards, interpreting recruitment metrics)?
- How are your digital marketing and social media campaign skills?

Digital fluency – behaviours

- Do you experiment with new tools and stay up to date on the latest recruitment tech trends?
- Do you use data to inform decisions and improve outcomes?
- Do you prioritize user-friendly digital experiences for both candidates and hiring managers?
- Do you balance tech adoption with a human-centred approach?

Commerciality – knowledge

- Do you understand the financial impact of vacant roles (or empty seats) on your organization?
- Can you articulate how TA contributes to revenue, productivity, or customer outcomes?
- Have you made sourcing decisions based on ROI or strategic value?
- Do you use business metrics (not just HR metrics) to communicate TA performance?
- Have you built a business case for investment in recruitment or proposed a strategic hiring initiative?

Commerciality – skills

- Do you have strong business acumen (understanding of financial drivers, operations and strategy)?
- Can you confidently manage and influence stakeholders?
- Do you perform ROI analysis and budget-conscious decision-making?
- Can you confidently build a business case and influence upwards?

Commerciality – behaviours

- Do you know how to align TA goals with business objectives?
- Can you speak the language of the business, not just HR?
- Do you make data-backed decisions with commercial outcomes in mind?
- Do you advocate for talent as a strategic enabler, not a cost centre?

Creativity – knowledge

- Have you created or contributed to a unique employer brand strategy that allows the firm to stand out among competitors?
- Do you look beyond traditional channels like LinkedIn to find talent?
- Have you assessed the candidate experience to check how personalized and human it is?
- Have you helped to support programmes to access non-traditional or overlooked talent pools?
- Do you challenge the status quo in your recruitment processes to keep things fresh and engaging?

Creativity – skills

- Can you tell stories to bring your employer brand to life?
- Do you feel comfortable creating content and designing campaigns?
- Do you develop programmes and pipelines (e.g. early careers, returnships)?

- Do you seek to solve problems creatively and innovatively using design thinking principles?

Creativity – behaviours

- Do you challenge standard practices and think outside the box?
- Do you tailor messaging to emotionally resonate with target audiences?
- Do you encourage experimentation and embrace failure as part of innovation?
- Do you strive for differentiation in a crowded talent market?

Consolidate your learning

Use the following checklist to consolidate your learning from this book.

Your sense of organization

- Do you have a strong understanding of the key environmental factors, such as technological, societal and economic trends that shape organizations and influence their recruitment strategy?
- Can you confidently explain the concept of being a Talent Value Leader and how you might be able to provide value by aligning recruitment strategies with broader business goals?
- Can you confidently explain the difference between reactive recruitment reporting and insight-led talent conversations, including the use of an external peripheral vision to anticipate trends and inform decision-making?

Your recruitment expertise

- Can you explain the differences between strategic WFP, recruitment forecasting, and operational recruitment planning?

- Can you outline the five functional TA activities with the ability to drive proactive recruitment strategies, i.e. sourcing strategy?
- Have you understood how nurturing near-miss candidates can plug the 'leaky bucket' and strengthen pipelines?
- Do you feel more confident about the opportunities and risks AI brings into HR and recruitment?
- Can you differentiate between equity and equality in talent selection?
- Have you shifted your view of onboarding as the beginning of talent development, not just an administrative step?
- Do you understand the balance between using technology and human oversight to create fair, future-ready hiring practices?
- Are you aware of how to use training data and guard against algorithmic bias, the possible pitfalls that prevent an ethical recruitment strategy?

Action planning for influencing recruitment strategy

Creating an action plan for influencing recruitment strategy can provide structure and clarity to your professional development. It can help you identify goals, set timelines, and break down what you want to know into discrete, manageable steps.

Use the template provided to set yourself some goals in relation to your development in TA and how you will seek to influence TA strategy in your organization. Remember that it is never too early to start questioning and challenging the way that things are done. Aim to set yourself at least three objectives and provide as much detail as possible when drafting your action plan and the specific goals within it. Three rows have been completed as examples.

TABLE 9.1 An action plan for continuous learning

What is your specific objective?	What is the current situation?	What do you need to explore?	How will you know when you have been successful?	Priority level	Due date
Develop a global mindset in TA and gain a global HR role	My experience is mostly UK focused. No involvement in international recruitment or understanding of global labour markets.	Research hiring trends in some of our key markets where our business operates. For example, we hire in France, Germany and the USA. Attend internal global meetings to gain exposure to global challenges.	Able to contribute an insight on a regional talent market during a recruitment strategy discussion or share a case study in a team meeting.	Medium	4 months
Improve digital fluency	Comfortable with basic ATS tasks but not confident using more advanced features or evaluating recruitment tech.	Shadow a recruitment business partner using CRM tools, AI screening, or digital sourcing platforms. Take a short course on emerging TA tech (e.g. via LinkedIn Learning).	Confidently use at least one new digital tool (i.e. sourcing) to support a live recruitment process and explain its benefits to the team or manager.	High	3 months
Build data fluency to support recruitment decisions	Limited experience using data in TA. Mainly reviewing reports without interpreting trends or influencing decisions.	Learn how to use tools like Excel or Power BI to analyse recruitment metrics (e.g. time to hire, source of hire). Understand what KPIs matter to the business.	Able to confidently present recruitment metrics in a meeting and explain what they mean and how they impact strategy.	High	2 months

Endnote

1   *Harvard Business Review* (2023) Transforming talent acquisition
    through the power of automation and artificial intelligence, 16 August,
    https://hbr.org/sponsored/2023/08/transforming-talent-acquisition-
    through-the-power-of-automation-and-artificial-intelligence (archived
    at https://perma.cc/QVE4-AMUA)
2   Srivastava, S (2025) AI in HR market to skyrocket to $14.08 billion
    by 2029, People Matters, https://www.peoplematters.in/news/
    hr-technology/ai-in-hr-market-to-skyrocket-to-1408-billion-by-2029-
    report-44274 (archived at https://perma.cc/GQ2X-XGTS)

Answers to 'What would you do?' exercises

This appendix gives suggested responses to the 'What would you do?' exercises included throughout this book. These exercises are designed to help you apply concepts in real-world scenarios and reflect on how you might approach practical challenges in a thoughtful, informed way.

Each answer offers an example of how a situation could be handled. They are not definitive solutions, but rather indicative responses meant to stimulate critical thinking and help you explore possible approaches.

You may find that your responses differ from these suggestions; that's completely normal. Check out what's different and:

1 Identify any gaps in knowledge.
2 Identify what you did differently that others can learn from.

WHAT WOULD YOU DO? NUMBER 1

You're concerned about the rapid adoption of AI in recruitment, while ensuring that human oversight remains at the forefront to protect the company from reputational risks. You've heard about other companies' AI implementations, which have raised significant ethical, legal, and reputational challenges. The business also expects you to ensure that inclusion is at the heart of this campaign and to consider soft skills and cultural fit. It is on-board with the concept of skills having a short shelf life and appreciates a 'can-do' attitude and growth mindset.

Take a few moments to read the following and reflect on how you might be able to use your influence to ensure that AI is implemented more responsibly:

- **Bias and fairness** – if the AI is trained on biased data, such as historical hiring trends or limited demographic representation, it could unintentionally disadvantage certain groups. For example, focusing heavily on technical skills may unintentionally overlook women or other underrepresented groups who possess the right balance of soft skills and cultural fit.
- **Diversity** – organizations that rely solely on AI without any human oversight risk the exacerbation of pre-existing biases in their workforces, particularly if the teams are predominantly male. AI could miss potential candidates who bring diverse perspectives and experiences, undermining diversity and inclusion goals.
- **Employer reputation** – if candidates perceive the process as biased or overly automated, it could harm the company's reputation, especially in a time when fairness, inclusivity, and transparency are valued. This could discourage diverse candidates from applying, potentially damaging your employer brand.
- **Discrimination risks** – without proper transparency or oversight, AI could unintentionally disadvantage marginalized groups, such as disabled or neurodivergent candidates. Discrimination may be hidden by the 'neutral' nature of the algorithm, making it harder to detect or address any issues.

The following actions can help you to position yourself as a trusted advisor:

Your actions	Considerations
1. Identify the risks	• Assess the potential risks of relying solely on AI. • Focus on issues like bias in AI algorithms, where AI might overlook candidates based on demographic data. • Check if there is an over-reliance on data points that miss soft skills and cultural fit which are crucial in your company.
2. Evaluate the impact on diversity	• Consider what might unintentionally perpetuate biases in your recruitment process. • Are underrepresented groups at risk of being overlooked? • How this could affect the diversity of your workforce and employer brand?
3. Suggest actionable solutions	• Run regular bias audits of the AI system to ensure it is trained on diverse and representative data. • Ensure transparency by clearly communicating to candidates how AI is used in the recruitment process. • Define a clear AI policy, including how candidates use AI to assist them. • Embed human oversight at key stages of recruitment, such as final candidate selection, to ensure decisions align with your organizational values, including cultural fit and soft skills.
4. Communicate the benefits of oversight	• Reframe oversight as a key strength, highlighting that human oversight ensures fairness, reduces risk of inequitable outcomes and improves the candidate experience by maintaining a personal, human-driven approach to hiring.

By balancing AI efficiency with human decision-making, you'll ensure that technology is an enabler of inclusivity, fairness, and transparency, strengthening your company's recruitment process while protecting its reputation.

WHAT WOULD YOU DO? NUMBER 2

If you're in HR, supporting TA, here's what you can do:

- Review event data: analyse which events led to strong applications and successful hires, and which didn't.
- Assess location alignment: compare event locations to actual hiring needs and open roles.
- Review event budget: compare the overall cost of events to the number of successful hires, ask the TA team to calculate the cost-per-hire by event to identify the return on investment.
- Challenge assumptions: use this data to prompt a review of future event investments and push for targeted, outcomes-focused TA engagement strategies.
- Show empathy: acknowledge concerns around employer brand while guiding the business to see the full picture, from brand visibility to pipeline conversion.
- Support TA's strategy: reinforce the importance of prioritizing events that deliver talent outcomes.

If TA is part of your remit, here's what you can do simultaneously:

- Present the story behind the data: share insights on where candidates are dropping off and how process inefficiencies may be the root cause.
- Show the full funnel: visualize data from event attendance through to hires to highlight quality versus quantity gaps.
- Empower the business: support business leaders to attend non-strategic events for brand exposure, while TA focuses efforts on strategic, high-impact locations.
- Show empathy and challenge constructively: recognize the value the business places on brand visibility, but guide them

to reframe their thinking around candidate location and recruitment outcomes:

○ Help them explore whether there's an unconscious bias toward hiring candidates based near the office, rather than focusing on where the best talent actually is. Invite them to consider: Are we prioritizing proximity over potential?

Future scope and driving continuous improvement:

- Position TA as a partner: shift the narrative from being order-takers to insight-driven advisors.
- Start to report on event ROI and compile an event calculator to approve on future events and budget spend.

This data-driven approach improves the quality of hires and candidate experience.

WHAT WOULD YOU DO? NUMBER 3

As an HRBP, you could actively support your TA colleagues by considering the following:

- Do job descriptions reflect the current and future digital and cultural demands? If not, collaborate with business leaders to update them accordingly.
- Can you share insights with your TA colleagues on how to assess cultural fit and help them understand what 'collaboration' or 'accountability' really looks like in your organization?
- Draw on real examples and help translate abstract culture into actionable hiring criteria.
- Are there recent high performers who embody the shift to digital and global thinking? Use them as benchmarks to help TA understand the traits to seek in the market to try to replicate.

This list is by no means exhaustive, but it provides a few key ideas to consider on your journey as a HR trusted partner.

WHAT WOULD YOU DO? NUMBER 4

Start with small, high-impact wins – don't start too big:

- Prioritize the standardization of basic processes, for example, job requisitions, interview steps, and feedback forms.
- Create simple and repeatable templates, you may wish to pick one business unit or a department or even a role type (e.g. critical roles) to pilot as an improvement.

Build trust with the business:

- Engage and run a quick discovery exercise or audit the recruitment processes to identify any areas of duplication or inefficiency (e.g. multiple interview steps).
- Talk to hiring managers to understand their pain points and expectations.
- Communicate a clear and simple vision – we're moving from ad hoc practices to a unified process that will reduce time to hire, raise the quality of candidates and reduce our overall recruitment costs.
- Present quick metrics to show inefficiencies (time to fill, dropout rate of diversity).

Define roles and responsibilities:

- Clarify who owns what in the recruitment process (TA, manager screens, TA drives timelines).
- Create a basic service level agreement or framework (SLA – 48 hours for CV feedback).

Introduce light technology:

- If there is no ATS, then start with basic Excel tracking, SharePoint, or free scheduling tools to show early improvements.
- Use survey tools (free) for candidate feedback to support your recommendations and improvements.

Create a TA playbook (start small):

- How to raise a requisition.
- Gain approval for a new role.
- Basic job advert copy.
- Interview best practice.
- Standard interview questions.
- Communicate playbook on SharePoint.

Measure and evolve:

- What new metrics will you introduce to track progress (e.g. time to hire, time to offer, enhanced diversity)?
- Communicate, communicate, and communicate success and achievements.

WHAT WOULD YOU DO? NUMBER 5

Question 1
You could provide the following data and insight to TA:

- Age profile of current employees – so we can see who is nearing retirement in the next five to ten years.
- Skills inventory – a breakdown of key skills across the business, highlighting which ones are held mostly by older employees.
- Turnover trends – to identify areas with high staff movement or hard-to-fill roles.
- Internal mobility and promotion data – to understand how often we fill roles from within.
- Succession planning data – to look at workforce gaps in the next three years.
- Workforce planning forecasts – to see which departments expect growth or change in headcount.

This information would help TA focus on roles and skills most at risk and make more informed decisions about hiring priorities and timelines.

Question 2

To reduce the risk of skills shortages and productivity gaps, you could do the following:

- Succession planning – identifying successor gaps for critical roles and developing hiring plans in response to potential gaps.
- Early career pipelines – expanding graduate, apprenticeship, or internship programmes to bring in new talent early.
- Improved internal mobility – helping employees move into new roles and develop their careers within the company.
- Regular workforce planning reviews – to keep plans aligned with business changes and adjust proactively.

WHAT WOULD YOU DO? NUMBER 6

You can do a basic free LinkedIn search with Boolean logic in the LinkedIn search bar.

Example: 'data analyst' AND SQL AND Tableau. Another platform, Github, is great for software developers and you can do a free search: Go to Git-Hub.com (archived at https://perma.cc/5BR5-Z33J). Use a search query like: language: Python location: 'New York' 'Software Engineer' NOT 'Java'.

WHAT WOULD YOU DO? NUMBER 7

A possible response is:

'I understand that you want to feel fully confident before making a final hiring decision. That said, we have already conducted two rounds of interviews, and this would prolong the process and potentially create a poor candidate experience. I am curious to understand what specific concerns you or the team are trying to address.

Can you provide me with the feedback following the first two rounds and identify the gaps that you are seeking to address now? I'm also concerned that creating further rounds of interviews will create inconsistency in the process.'

Listen to the stakeholder and insist on providing thorough feedback before bringing the candidate into another interview round.

> 'We can certainly progress this candidate, however, I will need to provide them with meaningful feedback and confirmation of the recruitment process to ensure we are providing them with a great experience.'

WHAT WOULD YOU DO? NUMBER 8

A possible response is:

> 'Thanks for raising this. I can see that you believe this person could be a great fit. However, we need to be mindful of how this decision could be perceived, and we are legally required to ensure we have a fair and equitable process. I am concerned about the potential implications of nepotism bias and how this might be perceived across the organization, particularly if our recruitment process is audited.
>
> Nepotism bias, where personal relationships influence hiring decisions, can significantly undermine the fairness and credibility of our recruitment process. It not only raises questions about transparency and equal opportunity but could also damage morale, trust, and our employer brand, both internally and externally.
>
> We currently have 30 candidates who are investing time and effort to go through a structured and competitive process. Offering a role outside of that process would compromise the integrity of the entire recruitment effort.
>
> If you genuinely believe this candidate is qualified, I'd strongly recommend they be encouraged to apply through the same process, and we can fast-track them to the assessment centre provided they meet the right benchmark. Here is a link to the online process, and I'd be grateful if you could ask them to complete this as soon as possible.'

Looking for another book?

Explore our award-winning books from global business experts in Human Resources, Learning and Development

Scan the code to browse

www.koganpage.com/hr-learning-development

Our Brand New HR Skills Series

All the knowledge and skills for your HR Career